Macroeconomics and the Development of Political Economic Theory

Macroeconomics and the Development of Political Economic Theory

Brett John Cormick,
B.A. (Mil.), B.Econ., M.A. Econ., Ph.D

The Pentland Press
Edinburgh–Cambridge–Durham–USA

First published in 1994
by The Pentland Press Ltd
1 Hutton Close
South Church
Bishop Auckland
Durham

British Library
Cataloguing-in-Publication Data

A catalogue record for this book
is available from the British Library

ISBN 1-85821-184-0

Typeset by Carnegie Publishing Ltd., 18 Maynard St., Preston
Printed and bound by Antony Rowe Ltd., Chippenham

Jennifer, James and Jordan

Table of Contents

Preface

The current state of most of the world's industries, as characterised by unemployment, is not good. The turmoil and turbulence that we have experienced in the financial markets since the 1970s, and the failure of various economic policies have been a great source of frustration, particularly to the non-professional economists. It is now almost fifty years since the Bretton Woods Agreement. It was partly motivated by a desire to prevent the depression of the 1930s occurring again. During this period the world economy and its industries have gone through a sea change. At the time of writing this forward there are many economists who are concerned that the efforts made to prevent a 1930s style depression have been in vain.

This book is about the development of the various macroeconomic theories which have been developed in order to understand the workings of economies and their industries, and to enable policy makers to develop and implement strategies which are designed to improve the welfare of individual members of society. In this excellent book, Dr Brett Cormick traces the development of the various macroeconomic theories, to the present day, which have been the foundations upon which politicians have made vitally important decisions affecting all of us.

Macroeconomic theory is very much an art rather than a science. With the growing use of mathematical and econometric models, many would not recognise this. Dr Cormick has lucidly described the development of the sundry schools, showing how they have built upon earlier ideas, and how they compare and contrast.

For me, the great value of this work is two fold. First, each area addressed is discussed in sufficient detail so that superficialities are put aside. Second, an aim of the author has been to whet our appetites, and therefore he has given great incentives to the reader to delve into each topic separately in the future. As a result, I believe that he has achieved a significant contribution to macroeconomics by producing a book which has a delightful balance between breadth and depth, and will encourage the study of the subject more deeply. As an introduction to macroeconomic theory the book is very appealing. As an aide-memoire of the key points in the development of the subject, it may become indispensable to students of economics.

Michael J. P. Selby, MSc, PhD, MBA
Department of Accounting and Finance
The London School of Economics

1

Introduction

The theoretical development of macroeconomic theory is usually interpreted as a complex synthesis of empirical analysis, combined with conventional time-additive conjecture, concerning utility expectations, which attempt to rationalise the perceived directions and aggregates of the economic system as a whole. It is a teleological concept, designed to provide answers to questions concerning strategic socioeconomic phenomena such as social welfare, the desirability of government economic intervention, the promotion of individual freedom, and the availability of choice, within the parameters of the appropriate political economic framework.

However, conventional macroeconomic theory tends to tolerate the convenient assumption that specific economic functions may be regarded as constants or alternatively as variables, in order to facilitate the diagnostic analysis of more broadly defined political economic phenomenon. Therefore essentially quantifiable key economic indicators such as inflation, the capacity for production, rates of growth, the distribution of output, and total expenditure among particular goods and services of firms may be designated as theoretical constants. Alternatively, a variable value may be imposed on these and other key indexes such as pricing levels and employment levels. Unfortunately there is clearly an absence of an accepted translation mechanism, such as a convex model of equilibrium, capable of making allowances for the discrepancies between economic theory and economic fact within this context.

This may be illustrated by the discussion of simultaneous equation models, which must be amended when the model recognises that behaviour depends on expectations which are rational. Since standard macroeconomic theory focuses on static models, this assumption subsequently removes the dynamic structure which is required for the real consideration of future implications. The structural equations for the endogenous variables at time t, contain expectation variables $_{t-1}x^e/1$, but do not facilitate a dynamic structure. It is therefore not only necessary to include current values of exogenous variables, but also a distributed lag on past values of exogenous variables. In this instance it is understood that exogenous variables constitute the process used in determining the values of z_t, which are not dependent on the process determining the endogenous variables y_t, thus y must not Granger-cause z, as past values of y_t are not determinants of z_t.

Thus contemporaneous random disturbances must be correlated within the structure, implying that exogenous factors are auto-regressively obedient, within the contemporaneous covariance matrix and may be expressed as:

$$By_t + \Gamma_1 (_{t-1}y^e/_{1,t}) + \Gamma_2 z_t = ut$$

However in order to restore the intemporal structure, so that the rational expectation solution reflects the entire future path of the economy, it is necessary to reflect endogenous variables at time t + 1 where expectational variables are $_{t-1}y^e/1, t + 1$.

$$By_t + \Gamma_1 (_{t-1}y^e/1, t + 1) + \Gamma_2 z_t = ut$$

Therefore any significant analysis of the theoretical development of macroeconomic doctrine, must be achieved with reference to the requirements of the underlying utility specification, of the political economic paradigm that the theory subscribes to. This premise may be illustrated within the context of the accepted conventional paradigms in classical macroeconomic theory, such as Orthodox economics, Neoliberal economics, Heterodox economics and Radical economics. Additionally, while preserving the relevant associations with the various legitimate peripheral interpretations, it is also possible to establish a credible insight into the true nature of the provenance and development of the political economy, and hence the relevant attendant macroeconomic theory.

Thus, by establishing an objective, chronological frame of reference, a comprehensive analysis of the axiomatic details of the more traditionally contentious political economic issues, inherent within the specific orientation of non-rational expectations and wage-price flexibility of Keynesian and Monetarist schools is facilitated. Further, a rational expectation theme is central to the Neoclassical movement, while the Neo-Keynesian emphasis on the money-wage or money price level of inflexibility and Supply-Side economics tends to reassign monetary and fiscal policy. The Neoclassical Orthodoxy is indicative of a 'real' theory of fluctuations, and also exhibits price-wage flexibility and rational expectations, although it is non-monetary in concept.

This process affords an insight into the development of macroeconomic theory as it relates to the political infrastructure, without the characteristic compromises and distortions, created by natural political economic prejudices, that constitutes the legacy of the majority of the academic elucidations of this essential social scientific discipline. Clearly there exists a tendency towards incomplete communications within the exogenous socioeconomic structure, and this is exacerbated by the consequential problems of co-ordination.

It is therefore necessary to proffer a rational analysis of the development of macroeconomic theory, devoid of nascent endogenous political bias, and philosophical interpretation, establishing instead a realistic framework for the examination of the fundamental issues causal to the sociopolitical macroeconomic evolution, and hence to facilitate a clearer picture of the provenance of the current economic environment. It is further proposed to resolve this investigation with a realistic appraisal of the theoretical foundations of the conventional paradigms, based on clinical observations of intemporal reality preferences, rather than the tempting distractions of academic convenience, that have served to distort the real utility of seminal macroeconomic reason, by reducing it to the superfluous and inevitably undermining the credibility and utility of the discipline.

This process may be observed through the issues separating the principle representatives of the major paradigms in macroeconomic theory, as they serve to illustrate the inherently political nature of this complicated and as yet, ill-defined economic discipline. Such issues tend to originate from the predominantly heterogeneous interpretations concerning the legitimacy of the sociopolitical substitutions and subsequently the discordant appreciations concerning the form of political economic matrix considered most desirable to deal with the prognostic issues. It is from this perspective that the major paradigms may be most effectively analysed, with a view to identifying the issues and origins relevant to determining the critical evolutionary discrepancies in the development of macroeconomic theory.

One of the more widely embraced paradigms in the discipline of macroeconomic theory is commonly referred to as Neoclassical economics.[1] A major exponent of this economic school of thought is Samuelson. This substantially orthodox economic doctrine is known as the Neoclassical synthesis, due to its origins in Classical or Mainstream economics. Samuelson claims that this is due mainly to the large scale adoption and implementation of Keynesian macroeconomic doctrine.[2]

Neoclassical economics may be interpreted through Samuelson's work to imply an orthodox, allegedly non-ideological representation of the modern capitalist system. Samuelson considers this system to be successful at achieving a perfunctory balance between the principal issues of material welfare and individual freedom, through a defined market mechanism, enjoined with the benevolent manipulative influence of government intervention, which is designed to alleviate deficiencies in the theory which are acknowledged to exist.[3]

Samuelson's definition of Neoclassical economics includes the incorporation of oligopolies in the orthodox, perfectly competitive model, established to produce a more realistic imperfect model, in an effort to simulate the reality of the market place. In this contrived version of economic reality, the individual uses the income he has received from production to affect the aggregate demand for goods

1 M. Olson Jr: 'What Is Economics' in *Modern Political Economy*, Allyn and Bacon, 1973, p. 19.
2 M. Kirzner: *The Economic Point Of View*, Sheed and Ward, Kansas, 1975, p. 143.
3 R. Ekelund Jr: *A History of Economic Theory And Method*, McGraw Hill, 1975, p. 314.

and services in the market. This is seen as an expression of the freedom of choice, which is conveyed in turn to the producers through the market, and acted upon in an attempt to maximise profits, by response to consumer demands.[4]

The predominant theme behind this rationale is the existence of a self-regulating market, which is capable of achieving equilibrium with less than full resource employment, and hence the requirement for government intervention in the form of fiscal and monetary manipulation in an attempt to aggregate consumer demand. Samuelson perceives the utilitarian purpose of Neoclassical economics as being representative of a managed economy which, in turn, is indicative of the capitalist system, with inherent consumer sovereignty , in spite of the obvious oligopolistic tendencies inherent within the economic superstructure. In this context, the producer is subordinate to the state, and the state is ultimately subordinate to the will of the individual. Thus, the expression of individual freedom and choice is central to the political economy of Samuelson's Orthodox economic paradigm.[5]

However, since the early 1970s, the most obvious practical illustrations of Samuelson's Neoclassical economy, or the actual economic system it seeks to interpret, have been the increasing and unabated incidence of unemployment, inflation, stagnant economic growth and a substantial worldwide recession to the point where theorists would be forgiven for suspecting we were entering a phase of macroeconomic anarchy. Samuelson is quick to point to the influences of exogenous variables to establish plausible long-term causal implications to exculpate the more obvious theoretical failings, but thus far, no satisfactory solution has been forthcoming from the Neoclassical theorists.

Therefore, it is reasonable to conclude that Neoclassical economics has been found wanting in both its interpretations of causal mechanisms, in intramurally defined product and factor market analysis,

4 W. J. Waters and E. Wheelwright: *University Economics. A Radical Critique,* ANZ Book Co., 1976, p. 23.
5 D. Fusfeld: *University of Michigan,* New York, 1972, p. 165.

and in the determination of the appropriate levels and instruments of fiscal and monetary intervention, necessary to explicate the contemporary economic impasse we are currently faced with. As a reaction to these intractable issues, economists who successfully subscribe to tenable alternative political economic dialectics are therefore regarded with renewed potential credibility.

Milton Friedman may be regarded as one such economist.[6] Friedman is a representative of the Neo-liberal paradigm, an alternative economic reasoning, developed as a reaction to the perceived inadequacies of Neoclassical economics.[7] Friedman's theories are essentially in accedence with the Orthodox paradigm as a viable political economic system, but viewed the socioeconomic context from a discordant perspective to those who supported the tenets of Samuelson. As such, the Neo-liberal economic paradigm is principally concerned with promoting the concept of individual freedom within predefined socioeconomic circumstances. To this end, traditional options such as Keynesian-orientated governmental intervention are rejected in favour of a viable structural alternative, namely the free market system. This may be interpreted as being conducive to an increase in the social welfare function and hence the propensity to promote individual liberty, as opposed to the utility of government intervention which is considered in this context to result in authoritarianism and potential economic instability.[8]

For Friedman and his pundits, freedom in the political and economic sense can only be attained within a competitive capitalist economic context, distinguished by the traditional characteristics of private enterprise, operating in free market conditions. Therefore the Neoliberal perception requires the presence of an effective and functional free market structure to facilitate a level of maximum economic efficiency and growth, while government involvement is restricted to an ancillary role, thus protecting the basis of individual economic freedom. However, by pragmatic necessity, there also exists an

6 Ibid. p. 165.
7 I. Kristol: 'A Disabled Science' in *The Age Monthly Review*, Vol.1, No.2, 1981, p. 3.
8 M. Friedman: *Introduction Capitalism and Freedom*, Chicago, 1962, p. 3.

appropriate requirement for government intervention which may be accommodated through the provision of law and order, contractual enforcement, monopoly control, property rights and other areas which serve to ensure the integrity and definition of the operating competitive system; thus promoting the effective functioning of the free market.[9] Government is therefore defined in this context as a means of promoting economic freedom, not of determining it, and is thus deprived of coercive powers by dispersal and deconcentration.

The principle role of the competitive capitalist system may therefore be interpreted as being the organising mechanism of the bulk of the economic activity, through private enterprise, to facilitate the operation of the free market via the voluntary cooperation of individuals within the economy. As such, enterprises are to be private and therefore representative of individuals with freedom of market entry and of any particular economic exchange. In keeping with the theme of market dominance to promote freedom, Friedman is then confronted by the issues of unemployment, inflation and economic growth. However, having opposed government fiscal macroeconomic measures, Friedman resorted to a revised Quantity Theory of Money to provide his response.[10]

The sophistry behind this theory held that substantial changes in the overall supply of money would indirectly produce noticeable variations in price and therefore output. Increases in output would result from increases in monetary stock, and as such, price stability would occur with full employment. Friedman held the belief that monetary policy was a powerful determinant in the attainment of economic stability when coupled with appropriate fiscal measures such as income redistribution through tax reforms, tariff abolition and the obviation of artificial privilege and market restrictions.[11] However, Friedman's central assertion that the quantity of money available is the principle determinant of the general price level, aggregate demand and national output, was not viewed as an economic

9 Ibid, p. 25.
10 R. Ekelund: Op Cit. p. 395.
11 M. Friedman: Op Cit. p. 35.

panacea by all those who differed from the orthodox economic approach.

Another paradigm was inevitably established, which went further in questioning the socioeconomic suitability of the orthodox approach, but additionally expanded the implications for the appropriate context for a political economic infrastructure. This alternative paradigm is known as Heterodox economics. Like the Neo-liberals it theoretically concurred with the basic Neoclassical concept of the viability of a competitive capitalist political economy as an economic base, but with a discordant and somewhat anomalous view of economic reality to that of Samuelson and Friedman. The major author of this paradigm is J K Galbraith, who regards Neoclassical economics as nothing more than an apologetic monopoly economy.[12] Galbraith's major objective is to reform the capitalist economic constitution because of the inherent tyranny he perceives to be endemic within the system, which was subsequently validated in the failings of the illustrative theoretical propositions and the attenuated flawed practical applications. These were predominantly embodied in an entity that Galbraith identified as the technostructure, which he felt commanded the economic destiny of the major corporations, which were in turn considered to be the dominant force within the political economy.[13]

For Galbraith the very concept of a market system is considered to be obsolete, as it fails to preserve the freedom of the individual because of the monopoly of social purpose imposed through the industrial system. The instrument of the repression of economic liberty, is transmitted through the technostructure of the large corporations, to the individual via the dependence effect which establishes a pattern of demand arising from production, rather than the orthodox concept of production arising from demand.[14]

The result of this perceived corporate economic manipulation of demand, is inevitably an unbalanced production function, characterised by an excess of private production and a deficiency of public

12 J. Gambs: *Evaluation: John Kenneth Galbraith*, Twayne, 1975, p. 105.
13 J. K. Galbraith: *Economics and the Public Purpose*, André Deutsch, 1974, p. 40.
14 D. Fusfeld: Op Cit. p. 169.

goods. The incongruous degree of economic power held within the corporations means that the real planning authority within the economy exists within the corporate technostructure, not the government, implying that the market economy is subjugated to the planned economy.[15]

Galbraith concludes that this political economic concept of inequitable corporate economic domination, is the underlying determinant of the current state of economic malaise, because it leads to price control through demand manipulation and inevitably inflation, both cost and demand, in addition to unemployment. The state is seen as a symbiotic organisation designed to supplement and respond to the needs of the contrived corporate planning system, because of the rewards for cooperation, and as such, it is not considered to be an effective instrument capable of combating economic inefficiencies.[16]

Galbraith therefore determines that the existing system constitutes a state of economic aberration, enhanced by producer sovereignty, dominated by corporate contrivances, where the technostructure within the corporation is identified as the ultimate authoritative force.[17] The State is thus reduced to a supplemental role within the market system which is representative of the agricultural, retail and service sectors; while the planning system has the economic and industrial power of the monopoly/oligopoly sector, which includes the major corporate firms, and is actually responsible for three quarters of the total economic output.

The theoretical conclusion of Galbraith's analysis points to an economic environment where the individual is actually a victim of the modern industrial system, with the line between corporate interests and the state interests being very thin. Galbraith believes the appropriate response to the deficiencies within the system is only to be found in the emancipation of the individual and the state.[18] Galbraith concludes that the public requires education in the inevitable possibility of structural change within the technostructure, and in the

15   J. K. Galbraith: Op Cit. p. 50.
16   J. K. Galbraith: Op Cit. p. 44.
17   D. Fusfeld: Op Cit. p. 1 70.
18   J. Oser: *The Evolution Of Economic Thought*, Syracuse University, New York, 1970, p. 364.

desirability of an implementation of a new socialism, where the public state is not controlled by the planning system and is actually retrieved for the public purposes.

It is considered that the implementation of these initiatives would eventually lead to substantial economic reforms such as wage and price fixing in the planning system, equality of income distribution, selective industrial nationalisation, greater market equality within the planning system, reduced planning system dominance, redistribution of technostructure power, increased percentages of resources channelled into public goods, monopolistic and oligopolistic restriction, the assurance that the planning system serves the public interest, and to ensure the sovereignty of the individual over the collective capitalists of the technostructure.[19]

However, while the first three illustrative conventional paradigms of Neoclassical, Neo-liberal, and Heterodox economics shared an essentially common view of the same political economic realities as quintessential economic parameters, although admittedly viewed from different socioeconomic perspectives, a fourth paradigm takes a radically different course.

The paradigm appropriately known as Radical economics, is also a reaction to conventional Neoclassical economics, and establishes its credibility as a complete alternative to the political economy of the market orientated capitalist system.[20] One of the major exponents of what may be described by its supporters as a theology of economic fundamentalism is Franklin. Franklin, like most radicals, bases significant conceptual derivations for his theories of Radical economics in the intellectual origins of the works of Karl Marx. However it would be inaccurate to claim that Franklin was totally influenced by Marx, especially in view of some of the more visibly acknowledged failings within the real application of his philosophical dialectic.

The major premise of Franklin's argument may be traced to a fundamental dissatisfaction with the Neoclassical economic system, and

19 J. Gambs: Op Cit. p. 115.
20 I. Kristol: Op Cit. p. 3.

subsequently the attendant capitalist system as a whole. Franklin believed in the historical dynamics of institutional change as an inevitability along the path towards economic liberation through a socioeconomic system participating, planning, and with a proprietary interest in the resources of the economy. This process is fundamental to the primary issue of the inevitable quest for an equality of income distribution.

Radical economics differs from the orthodox in that it is an inter discipline with less emphasis on the market and increased concentration on coordinating mechanisms operating through collective participatory planning mechanisms.[21] The premise of a congruent distribution of wealth is also afforded great importance, while incorporating a wholesale rejection of the concept of competitive individualism of capitalism as being incompatible within the altruistic framework of radical ideals.

Franklin's concerns are formulated through the implementation of policies designed to redistribute control of the economic destiny of the political economy through the socioeconomic infrastructure and through the regulation of corporations with monopolistic proclivities, in order to circumscribe capitalist domination; and the redefinition of the concept of economic surplus as an aid to increasing the aggregate level of social welfare. The labour process is also revalued to the standards of the social-economic structure rather than as a commodity, and economic growth is rationalised to deter gratuitous waste and superogatory economic growth and expansion.

The radical paradigm also offers an alternative solution to the conundrums of economic inefficiencies, as did the representatives of the previous alternative paradigms, however Franklin reduces the issues of unemployment and inflation as being intrinsic features of the capitalist system per se, claiming that they are the inevitable results of capitalist style economic development.

The radical explanation of the deficiencies of the system originate with the state, which is not regarded as an independent or realistically representative authority, due to industrial monopolistic influences,

21 Ibid, p. 4.

which in turn engender the establishment of large deficits necessary to provide public utilities. The use of taxation by the state can be seen as being politically undesirable, and therefore a wage and price spiral is created, resulting in severe unemployment, unless the system is able to expand, however inflation is considered to be the price for obtaining finance for expansion through deficits.[22]

For Franklin other contributing factors to the undesirability of the orthodox capitalist Neoclassical economy include imperialism, racism, environmental abuse, alienation of workers, income inequality, the values of the existing system of the market and an intractable status quo.[23] Neoclassical economics is seen as being ideologically biased towards a static equilibrium position and the justification of a system that does not allow for human emancipation through its irrelevance and invalid logic models which too often produce practical failures. Therefore radical economics is seen as a political-economic alternative to sustain the interests of the individual in an economic environment of socioeconomic interaction through qualitative change in the historical destiny of social development.[24]

Therefore having briefly touched on the significant alternative macroeconomic paradigms, it is possible to conclude that within the context of a clearly rationalised investigation, of the appropriate relevance of the political economic consequences, there would appear to be a compromise in utility and integrity. Clearly such obvious discrepancies and incongruities in theoretical perspectives, of what is ostensibly the same fundamental environment of contention, is cause for some concern when the implications are as significant as they are for macroeconomics as a field of practical political application. It is therefore necessary to examine the provenance of the political economic influences, congruent to the disparities, to facilitate a comprehensive insight into the development of macroeconomic theory as an integral force in the development of the political economy.

22 R. Edwards: 'A Radical Approach To Economics' in *American Economic Review*, 1970. p. 356.
23 Ibid, p. 356.
24 W. J. Waters: Op Cit: p. 21.

2

The Pre-Capitalist Economy

The pre-capitalist system is a term used to describe the period of political economic history prior to the advent of capitalism or the capitalist system. This is actually a convenient generalisation aimed at describing a structure where productive resources are privately owned and their allocation to productive activity is determined by the market mechanism, which is the coordinating instrument of capitalist theory.

The term pre-capitalist economy is usually employed to describe economies predating the rise of capitalism in Western Europe. However, it is also employed to refer to so called primitive economies, which continue to exist well after the ascendancy of the capitalist system in the developed world. It is important to note at this point that this does not in any way imply any inevitability in the development of these economies into capitalist market-orientated models, despite the assumptions to be found in some literature in the field of development economics. In essence it reflects an embryonic precursor of the modern capitalist political economy without the strictures of a historical imperative.

Writers such as Polanyi[25] have extensively analysed economic activity in the great societies of antiquity and the societies of the Western world during the Middle Ages up to and including the time of the Industrial Revolution. Interestingly, the one common denominator, evident in all of these antediluvian economies is that they did not rely on the market mechanism to orchestrate economic activity.

25 G. Dalton: *Primitive, Archaic and Modem Economies, Essays of Karl Polanyi*, Doubleday, Anchor books, 1968. p. xxxiiii.

As it has been previously stated, the market mechanism integrates or coordinates a capitalist economy in the sense that it is the instrument by which resources are brought together and allocated to appropriate fines of production in response to the motivation of profitability.

It is also obvious that in spite of the clearly defined role of the market mechanism in most modern capitalist economies there may also exist a propensity to concede to pressures to embrace the establishment of a welfare state infrastructure. Despite the fact that market forces are over-ridden in various ways, it is generally accepted that the market remains the basic mode of integration.

However, this was not the case in pre-capitalist economies. To use Heilbroner's description;

> They were subsidiary to the great processes of production and distribution rather than integral to them; they were above the critical economic machinery rather than within it.

Additionally according to Dalton:

> Where markets existed, they were most frequently confined to a few produced items, the sale of which did not contribute appreciably to the livelihood of producers or sellers. Markets were contained, and nowhere created an economy wide system.[26]

It is historically evident that at no time prior to the second quarter of the nineteenth century were markets any more than a subordinate feature in any socioeconomic collective. This indicates that the concept of a structure organised on the basis of individual attainment had not yet been established, and that a separate self-contained economic function had not yet been extracted from the prevalent socio-political context.

It would appear that the motivation of reciprocity, social approbation and competition were more relevant in this subsistence milieu, than the more familiar incentives of individual acquisition, remuneration

26 Ibid, pg xiii.

for labour and the restriction of labour to the unavoidable minimum.[27] Evidently, this then implies that the economy was subjugated to an extension of the socioeconomic relationships of the individual. Therefore the individual is not seen to protect his autonomous interest in the possession of material goods in this context; he acts only to ensure his sociopolitical standing, his socio-communal claims, and his socioeconomic assets. Material goods are valued only insofar as they serve this end.

The result of this process is that it further serves to divorce the production function and the distribution matrix from specific economic interests related to the possession of goods; however these processes are obviously still undertaken to a limited extent due to socioeconomic incentives or non-economic motives.[28] Given that the word economy is indicative of a domain of activity, the practice of economy is therefore the undertaking of the production and distribution of goods and services within this context.

The evidence clearly indicates that in pre-capitalist economies, the institutions, used in the broadest sense, through which goods and services were produced and distributed were conceived as an integral part of the existing sociopolitical convention; with the economy functioning as a by-product of kinship and the inevitably political and religious obligations. The concept of reciprocity is therefore central to understanding this process, as it explains a general category of socially obligatory gift-giving. As such it is simply a material expression of these socially cohesive relationships that we call friendship and kinship. This can be further expanded to include the concept of redistribution, which consists of transactions which are payments to, and disbursements by, a central political authority.

Obviously both practices of reciprocity and redistribution exist in our contemporary market-orientated society, the latter increasingly so with the greater role of central authority, just as markets existed in pre-capitalist societies, however there is no longer any substantially

---

27 K. Polanyi: *The Great Transformation,* reprinted in Dalton, Op Cit. pg 20.
28 Ibid, pg 7.

dominant integrative influence, as the pre-capitalist economies would tend to indicate. From this perception we may readily conclude that administrative planning, command, and tradition operate effectively as a basic coordinating mechanism, however it is rather more difficult to understand the concept of the market as a coordinating mechanism.[29]

In a theoretically contrived market system, all productive resources are owned privately. The owners of the resources sell the utility of these resources to business firms who in turn use them to produce goods and services. The purpose of this activity is to yield resource owners income with which they may purchase goods and services. Within the theoretical confines of a pure market system this is the only way people may earn income and hence actually obtain the means by which they may purchase goods and services.

Business firms in turn produce goods and services and sell them to the consumers. The exchange nexus in each case is clearly defined as the market. A market may therefore be defined in turn as the point of contact between buyers and sellers of a particular resource, that is to say a resource market, or in the instance of a particular good or service, a produce market. Consequently in a market system there are as many individual resources and product markets as we care to identify or define as different individual resources or products. In each case there will exist a quantifiable demand and supply relationship. Therefore, it is implicit in the underlying concept of a market system that individuals seek to maximise satisfaction in their role as buyers in product markets and revenues in their role as suppliers of resources they own in resource markets, with firms attempting to maximise profits throughout the process.

Arising out of the great number of buyer-seller interactions in individual resource and product markets will be a pattern of production and distribution of goods and services. That is, in each product market the demand-supply relationship will result in a price and a level of production of the particular product. The sum of these gives

29 Heilbroner: *The Wordly Philosophers*, pp. 17–18. (See also Heilbroner's *The Makinq of Economic Society*, pp. 21–25).

a matrix of production for the economy as a whole. In each resource market the demand-supply relationship will result in an appropriate price and quality of the particular resource traded. The value of a resource together with the quantity of it an individual owns will determine personal incomes and hence purchasing power over goods and services produced. Consequently, given the distribution of ownership of resources, the operation of resource markets will determine the distribution of income in the system and hence the distribution of goods and services produced in the system.

It is therefore obvious that just as the mechanisms of pre-capitalist tradition are able to produce a pattern of production and distribution, so too can the forces of the market. The question of planning versus the market is a central one in political economic theory. One of the key differences between the two is that planning involves the translation of the conscious individual design of the planning authority into, in the extreme case, individual receipts of goods and services. A pure market system on the other hand, translates individual demands for specific goods into economic decisions concerning prices and outputs.

This process may be described as the non-purposeful achievements by private persons of a social-economic purpose. Non-purposeful in this context implies that there is no overall conscious human design about the use of resources and, more specifically, those who act in conformity with market forces are not necessarily aware of the consequences of their actions for the socioeconomic environment as a whole.

We may therefore conclude that the initial distribution of proprietorial interests is crucial because it determines the distribution of income. Additionally, consumer demand, for goods and services, to which firms respond, is only effective if it is substantiated by income; therefore in this context the distribution of income is of primary importance in the determination of the pattern of production of goods and services. Obviously, the implications of these fundamental pre-capitalist economic insights are therefore of significant interest when considering the political economic development of economic theory, as they set the stage for the evolution of the socioeconomic context within which the revolution in economic dynamics occurred.

3

The Economic Revolution

The economic revolution responsible for the essence of the change associated with the actual advent of the economic system which was to be known as capitalism, was a result of three fundamental changes from the pre-capitalist economy. These changes were not short term socioeconomic aberrations, but represented a significant transposition of the sociopolitical philosophy prevalent at the time, and were to have economic, political and social implications for centuries to come.

The essential focus of the new economic order concentrated on the acceptance by the socioeconomic assemblage, of the assumption that market forces took over the task of regulating economic interest. This new attitude towards economic occupation demonstrated that by necessity, the quest for economic gain was a legitimate form of social enterprise, indicating an acceptance of a high degree of monetary complicity in authentic economic activity.

The acceptance of the market as a regulating force was the critical step in this stage of macroeconomic development, with the succeeding features representing co-requisites of the change, rather than the essence of the transformation. According to Hughes:

> The competitive market in the capitalist society replaced the rules of the medieval town. In medieval England and later under Tudor and Stuart regulations regarding labour and manufacturing a place was made, within the fabric of ordered English life, for new industry to be introduced and to grow. Now, it is a misconception to consider either the medieval orders of the Tudor rulers as the framework of a perfectly stagnant and unchanging economy. But the amount of change was constricted

19

by the existence of regulations against free mobility of productive factors, and the pace of change could be fixed by
administrative methods. What the lapse of these restrictions
meant was that the order of privilege and tradition was sup-
planted by the infinitely more flexible order of the market
place.[30]

The essential theoretical requirement justifying the supposition that
market forces were the major instrument regulating economic activity,
was reduced to a single premise; that all of the contributing elements
introduced into the production function and the subsequent distribution
of goods and services, had to be injected into the market and treated
as if they were commodities to be bought, sold and exchanged.
As Preston points out:

The feudal tie that bound the serf to that land and consigned
a portion of his produce to his lord had to be broken so that
the former could offer his labour, not for protection and security, but for a price, wages, with which he could afford in
the market. Land would need to lose its political meaning as
the basis for lordship and become available at its price, rent,
to those who would put it to productive use. Wealth, instead
of being used for hospitality, ostentation and worship, would
need to be loaned or offered at its price, interest, or employed
for profit, and the religious strictures against usury, a deroga-
tory implication concerning any form of interest would need
to disappear. The relation of all three of these, labour, land
and capital, to the social and political system would have to
be altered in order to fit their new definition as commodities
in the market.[31]

It is obvious that the precondition for the market system to evolve
into a capitalist framework was the acceptable interpretation of natural

30 J. Hughes: *Industrialisation and Economic History, Theses and Conjectures*, McGraw-Hill,
1970. p. 50.
31 N. S. Preston: Politics, *Economics and Power*, Macmillan, 1967. p. 20.

resources, human effort and technology, as legitimate factors of production. This represents a significant development in socioeconomic theoretical maturity, as factors of production were no longer allocated in accordance with kinship, tribal, religious or political rights and obligations, but became freely tradeable in their respective markets.

In modern economic terminology, these features are more commonly referred to as land, labour and capital. The quantity of these goods traded, and their tangible transaction value is determined, as for any commodity, by demand and supply forces. This may serve to imply that there is an obvious synergy between the operation of resource or factor markets to that of commodity or product markets.

Polanyi responded to this development by noting simply:

> All along the line, human society had become an accessory of the economic system.[32]

It is arguable that many of the inconsistencies and unresolved issues of contemporary capitalist societies may be related in some degree to this issue.

The origins of the events which constituted the context for this reformation, are among the great enigmas confronting economic historians. When reference is made to the rise of capitalism it is a reference concerned essentially with Britain in the last several decades of the eighteenth, and first decades of the nineteenth centuries. The rationale for the substantial metamorphosis that took place is to be found in what Heilbroner once described as an immense coalition of events.

However, perhaps the circumstance most immediately responsible was the Industrial Revolution. Certainly it established the transformation of a basically agrarian and subsistence level commercial socioeconomic system into one where industrial manufacture was central to economic enterprise. The effect of the machine was dramatic. Dalton in fact seems to regard the rise of capitalism and the Industrial Revolution as one and the same thing.

---

32 K. Polanyi: Op Cit. pg 75.

Polanyi went further to illustrate this concept by adding further emphasis:

> But how shall Revolution itself be defined? What was its basic characteristic? Was it the rise of the factory towns, the emergence of slums, the long working hours of children, the low wages of certain categories of workers, the rise in the rate of population increase, or the concentration of industries? We submit that all of these were merely incidental to one basic change, the establishment of a market economy, and that the nature of this institution cannot be fully grasped unless the impact of the machine on a commercial society is realised. We do not intend to assert that the machine caused that which happened but we insist that once elaborate machines and plant were used for production in a commercial society, the idea of a self-regulating market was bound to take shape.[33]

Clearly the widespread implementation of specialised production machinery in an agrarian society, with commercial transaction facilities, must produce significant effects in the fundamental structure of the socioeconomic function. Such a society must by nature consists of agriculturalists and of merchants who in turn purchase and promote the produce of the land for trade. Production with the benefit of specialised, expensive capital equipment and plant can be incorporated into such a society only by making it incidental to the function of commerce through buying and selling.

In this socioeconomic proposition, the merchant is the only individual available for this undertaking and as such he is entitled to do so to the extent that this process does not involve the sustaining of a diminution of capital through the proceedings. He will transact the goods in the same manner in which he would otherwise merchandise them to those who demand them; but he will procure them in a different manner, namely not by buying them ready-made, but by purchasing the necessary labour and raw materials. The combination

---

33 Ibid, pp. 40–41.

of these factors of production, according to the merchant's instruction, plus a necessary interim hiatus which is necessary to the production function, amounts to the new product. Clearly this is not an exclusive description of an elementary domestic industry in an embryonic format, but is typical of most examples of industrial capitalism, including that of our time. It is also clear that important consequences for the socioeconomic system follow from this event.

Given the inevitability that elaborate capital goods are expensive, they are therefore not commercially efficient unless significant quantities of goods are produced. Manufacture of such goods may proceed without a loss only if the vent of the goods is reasonably assured, and if production need not be interrupted for want of the primary products necessary to nourish the machines. For the merchant this means that all factors involved must be accessible, that is, they must be available in the required quantities to anybody who is prepared to pay for them. Unless this condition is guaranteed, production through the facility of specialised machines is too precarious to be undertaken, both from the point of view of the merchant who speculates his capital and of the socioeconomic group as a whole, which is dependent upon continuous production for incomes, employment and provisions.

By comparison, in an exclusively agrarian economy such conditions would not naturally be given, they would by nature need to be contrived. However the fact that they would be constituted gradually in no way alters the significant nature of the changes involved. The transformation implies a change in the very motive of action on behalf of the members of the socioeconomic assemblage. Therefore the underlying psychology of the system is transformed from the motivation of subsistence to that of gain. All transactions are interpreted as capital negotiations, and these in turn require that a medium of exchange be introduced into every articulation of industrial life. All incomes must be derived from the transaction process, and whatever the principle source of an individual's income, it must be regarded as ultimately resulting from the bargaining process.

No less is implied in the simple term market system by which we designate the institutional pattern described. But the most eloquent peculiarity of the system as a political economic entity lies in the fact that, once it is established, it must be allowed to function without outside interference. Profits are not guaranteed under these circumstances, and the merchants must make their revenues according to the specific nuances of the market. Prices in this context must be allowed to regulate themselves, and as such a self-regulating system is integral to the political economy of the market economy. Additionally, in a community model with public expenditure set by voting, with migration between communities, they may become heterogeneous in competition and therefore inefficient. Equilibrium occurs when the peer group effect is neither stronger nor weaker, because of the externality of migration inefficiencies.

The transformation to this system from the initial proposition of the primitive political economy is so complete that it resembles more a mutation than any progression that may be expressed in terms of a quantifiable continuity of growth and development. Why industrialisation made its decisive appearance in Britain in the second half of the eighteenth century is a much more elaborate question which will not be confronted here. Nor is it necessary to examine the extent to which other forces influenced the advent of the market economy and what their causal relationships were with the process of industrialisation. Heilbroner discusses several of these in detail, including the issue which remains the subject of so much contention to date, namely the effect of the spread of Protestantism.

However the issue remains that an accumulation of forces revolutionised economic activity and altered the traditional structural attitudes associated with it. The net result was the emergence of a political economic order where survival was henceforth accomplished neither by custom nor command, but by the free action of profit-seeking individuals bound together only by the market itself. This system was to be called capitalism.

4

Classical Political Economy

The concept of classical political economy has in its provenance the central principle of economic liberalism or laissez-faire, as espoused by the writings of certain philosophers of the eighteenth and the early nineteenth century. Few countries have ever been more dominated by a prior doctrine than Britain was by the process of laissez-faire political economics in the early nineteenth century.

It is of significant relevance that the subsequent process which lead to the dismantling of the obstructive and inefficient mercantilist controls and regulations, and hence the eventual establishment of a free market economy, was largely the result of the theories of the classical political economists. In fact, so significant was this period in the development of macroeconomic theory that Robins claims:

> It is no exaggeration to say that it is impossible to understand the evolution and the meaning of western liberal civilisation without some understanding of classical political economy.[34]

Polanyi states that:

> Economic liberalism was the organising principle of a society engaged in creating a market system. Born as a mere penchant for non-bureaucratic methods, it evolved into a veritable faith in man's salvation through a self-regulating market.[35]

Clearly this is a colourful, if somewhat simplistic, description of the origin of the doctrine, however it is considered that it may be

---

34 L. Robbins: *The Theory of Economic Policy in English Classical Political Economy*, Macmillan, 1952. p. 4.
35 K. Polanyi: Op Cit p. 135.

more accurately attributed to a reaction to the well documented
ineffectiveness, incompetence and corruption of eighteenth century
governments; and certainly it was also in part a response to the fact
that from about 1750 material progress fairly obviously stemmed
from individual initiative, that is from the activities of individuals
with entrepreneurial interests.

Within this context, the only significant influence attributable to
any clearly characterised socioeconomic institution must be interpreted as a retarding or restraining factor in relation to entrepreneurial
propensities. Additionally, the origin of the principle of laissez-faire
may also be traced to two eighteenth century schools of thought
which were brought together and extended by writers who have since
been labelled the first economists.

The first school of thought, associated particularly with the names
Locke and Hume, was concerned primarily with the concept of individualism. The second, associated particularly with Rousseau and
Bentham, concentrated on the notions of equality and altruism and
may be regarded as being representative of the basis of the political
economic ideals of socialism and democratic egalitarianism.

These apparently opposite rationalisations were reconciled in the
notion of a divine harmony perpetuated between the motivations of
private gain and the pursuit of public advantage. Natural laws were
discerned whereby individuals protected their own interests, while
operating under the conditions of self determination, always tending
to promote the general interest simultaneously. The essence of the
implication for classical political economists was the impression of
the presence of a natural divine harmony. This was eventually
replaced by a rational scientific basis, but the implication was the
same; unfettered private action and enterprise would promote the
greater good of the whole.

It is neither practical or appropriate to consider the views of all
the classical economists at this point, as diverging views on essentially
minor considerations, when viewing this context of macroeconomic
development in its embryonic stage will serve only to distract from
the fundamental issue of investigation, rather than to facilitate its

disclosure. Therefore, it is considered that the writings of Adam Smith are appropriate to illustrate the essential developments in macroeconomic theory at this point in its teleological progression.

Adam Smith's view of the acceptable role of government in economic activity was derived from his desire to constitute, not simply a suitable environment for economic enterprise, but also an instrument for political economic development and socioeconomic progress. As such, Smith believed in a pragmatic non-interventionist government policy, which while not subscribing to the economic anarchy of a dogmatic laissez-faire system of government policy, did draw a boundary distinguishing certain practices of government as being desirable or unacceptable to the socioeconomic welfare function.[36]

To this end Smith sought to condemn specific government practices as being contrary to the natural order of divine harmony in political economic development. Examples may be used to illustrate this point which include such restrictive mercantilist regulations as Settlement and Apprenticeship laws, bounties on exports, restraints on imports, legal monopolies, laws of Succession hindering free trade, prohibition of foreign trade, laws sheltering industry from competition, unproductive government expenditure, and most significantly for Smith, governmental manipulation and interference with the market mechanism.[37]

The majority of these economic regulations were designed by the political authorities of the time, who were of a low standard, and as a group substantially comprised of aristocratic cliques determined to encourage the status quo through mercantilistic non-progressive legislation.[38] The benefits of this system tended to extend themselves primarily to the upper classes and to a limited extent the merchants, rather than to the development of the general socioeconomic group as a whole.

However Smith also acknowledged that the natural order of economic development contained inherent factors which were potentially

36 B. Richmond: *Political Economy and Comparative Systems*, 1985. p. 3.
37 R. Heilbroner: 'The Wonderful World of Adam Smith', *The Wordly Philoophers*. p. 57.
38 J. Viner: 'Adam Smith and Laissez-Faire', *Journal of Political Economy*, Volume 35. 1927. p. 221.

detrimental to the principles of social welfare if left unhindered.[39] He therefore concluded that government activity could be interpreted as beneficial and in concert with the natural order only when it resulted in a substantial benefit to the general welfare, and was to be regarded as an undesirable interference if the general welfare was decreased.

Smith outlined his concept of the extent to which it was acceptable for the government to play a role in the economy. This did not include the incorporation of completely free trading regulations, as this utopian ideal was realistically not feasible, given the opposing interests visible between the welfare needs of society and the profit requirements of the manufacturing sector in general.

As Smith believed:

> People of the same trade seldom meet together, even for merriment and diversion, but the conversation ends in a conspiracy against the public, or in some contrivance to raise prices.[40]

The correct role of government was seen in principle as compensating for the shortcomings of the invisible hand in the market mechanism[41] providing considerations for an increase in social welfare by the provision of facilities private industry would be unwilling to provide due to a lack of a profitable incentive. To this end there exist three legitimate circumstances identified by Smith which validate government intervention within the economy.

The first was the duty to provide protection against external violence and invasion by other nations in the form of military security.[42] To this end it proved necessary to sanction certain regulations, which while not conducive to economic prosperity, were desirable in consideration of defence requirements. Some examples include the Navigation Act, bounties on essential goods and limited foreign trade concessions.

---

39 Ibid. p. 217.
40 R. Gill: 'The Evolution of Modern Economics', *Classical Economics*, Prentice Hall, 1967.
41 R. Heilbroner: Op Cit. p. 52.
42 R. Lekachman: *Adam Smith, A History Of Economic Ideas*. McGraw Hill, 1959. Chapter 4.

The administration of justice was also a role deemed appropriate for the government.[43] This was required to protect members of society from perceived injustice or oppression by other members of the same society. It was also to include enforcement of contracts, protection from fraud and to promote natural liberty in consideration of social justice.

Finally, there was a requirement for government entities to provide public utilities.[44] This included facilities which were to demonstrate considerable utility in collective and individual application, but were clearly beyond the means of the individual to provide. For example, highways, bridges, canals, harbours, and schools. These utilities all resulted in an increase in social welfare, external to those associated with an autonomous market mechanism.

Smith also condoned a limited range of mercantilistic regulations due to the pressures of economic realities, which proved desirable although not ideologically convenient. These included the restrictions of interest rates to five per cent, the provision of protection for infant industries where the product was considered to be in the national interest, limited retaliation against discriminatory foreign tariffs and restricted discriminatory taxes.[45]

Smith was therefore able to identify and substantiate theoretical conditions to support his concession to facilitate governmental intervention within the economy. The basic premise was that the natural laws of economics, which were originally established as originating through divine design, were perhaps more appropriately attributable to more familiar causes.[46]

This theory ideally suited Smith's optimistic view of the provenance of the economic system and the ultimate objective of the same. He argued that an absence of government interference, inevitably led to a liberal system conducive to an increased state of natural liberty

43 R. Romano and L. Leiman: 'Adam Smith's Wealth of Nations' in *Views On Capitalism*, Glencoe, 1975. p. 7.
44 M. Blaug: *Adam Smith: Economic Theory In Retrospect*. Heinemann, Chapter 2, 1968. p. 59.
45 R. Lekachman: Op Cit. p. 98.
46 Ibid, p. 89.

and therefore enhanced harmony with the natural order of economic affairs. Such a system would therefore create an optimisation of socioeconomic welfare and thus ultimately benefit the political economic infrastructure as a whole.

However, Smith also pointed out that the natural order did not extend to all aspects of the economic environment and was often imperfect, subjective or counter productive.[47] These circumstances were labelled natural conflicts and were to be negated by limited and predetermined government responses, thus reconfirming a state of natural harmony as a statistical aggregate of reality. This created a reactive role for government occupation in clearly defined areas of interaction, while terminating those seen as superfluous to the orderly operation of natural forces.

It is clear that there are obvious parallels between this optimistic interpretation of the natural order and that is demonstrated in the theory of the market mechanism.[48] As the economic system is considered to be divinely designed and therefore incorporates an inherent propensity for harmonious operation, it was considered logical that a market free of interference would naturally find its own level of prices, wages, profits and production. This premise was justified on the grounds that an automatic mechanism or Smith's invisible hand, was the appropriate instrument of natural harmony designed to bring the market back into equilibrium.[49]

In this fashion the market was defined as a potentially self regulating organism capable of the orderly provision of socioeconomic requirements, functioning through the catalyst of supply and demand. Therefore the theory asserts that the market itself was capable of satisfying all needs if left in isolation, because it guaranteed producers would supply goods to satisfy consumer demands at a price commensurate with market levels. This implies that government interference is to be avoided, in order to enable a free market to operate; however a degree of government control was also necessary to ensure

47   J. Viner: Op Cit. p. 218.
48   R. Heilbroner: Op Cit. p. 67.
49   R. Lekachman: Op Cit. p. 92.

competition was unrestricted by dealing with aberrations in the theory such as monopolies.

Another theoretical justification for his premise of government non-intervention existed in Smith's *Laws of Population and Accumulation*.[50] Smith stated that man's natural avarice could be beneficial to the socioeconomic matrix as a whole, if man was allowed to accumulate material gain through his own self interest. By following his egocentric instincts of self benefit, all of society would eventually be better off if the accumulated capital was allowed to grow unhindered, as this could be turned into machinery which would allow for the crucial division of labour, thus expanding the propensity of the socioeconomic productive capacity.

In this manner the social welfare function would increase and as wages increased commensurately, therefore the number of workers would increase because Smith saw men as an economic factor of production, with a regulated demand like other commodities. Freedom of entrepreneurial skills and ambition was an obvious requirement for such a theory to perform effectively, and as such, government taxes designed to destroy capital accumulation were to be avoided as a prerequisite for the effective operation of this system; however government sponsored programmes incorporating aspects of public health, safety and education were required to maintain an increased population base.

Therefore Adam Smith's system of economic freedom was clearly not, as some have implied, one of virtual economic anarchy. He was not a doctrinaire advocate of laissez-faire. He was however, the first to argue in a comprehensive way the case for the market and he laid the foundations of a system of thought that was to prevail for nearly a century. It therefore comes as no surprise that the paradigm established by Adam Smith was expanded upon by subsequent writers in the first half of the nineteenth century. The most notable of these were Thomas Malthus and David Ricardo, writing in the first two decades of the century, with J R McCulloch, Nassau Senior and John Stuart Mill, writing in the second quarter.

50 R. Heilbroner: Op Cit. p. 62.

Ricardo, like Smith, believed in the existence of natural economic laws, which it was the professional duty of the political economist to discover. The laws Ricardo formulated however, did not present such an optimistic picture of the world as those discerned by Smith. Ricardo interpreted the process of economic development as intrinsically favouring the landowners rather than the capitalists or wage-earners whose profits would eventually be diminished and wages reduced to subsistence levels. But gloomy though his predictions were, there were no recommendations advocating interference with the laws by which these events would follow, and indeed he was a vigorous opponent of the Corn Laws which prevented free trade in corn.

Malthus, like Smith, also subscribed to the view that the economic system was divinely designed, but in discerning the laws of the system disagreed, though for different reasons, with Smith's optimistic view of the direction the system was taking. While many of his views, especially those regarding the Poor Laws, which followed from his theory of population, represented a laissez-faire standpoint, his defence of the traditional English class structure and the landlords in particular, lead him to support the Corn Laws. The problem is that neither Ricardo nor Malthus ever really confronted or qualified the general question of government intervention; one cannot find in their writings a general statement on this issue. With the odd exception however, their views may be generally described as supporting the laissez-faire principle.

In contrast, McCulloch and Senior whose writings were influenced by the turbulent socioeconomic events following a generation of substantial economic and social disruption, arising out of the conditions of an early industrial society, refocused their attention, to investigate the changing political economic climes within this elusive context. The central theme tended to elaborate on controversies arising out of the conditions of an early industrial society, over matters such as tariffs, the Poor Laws, factory conditions, education etc. Clearly, economists in this era could hardly avoid the broader questions which Malthus and Ricardo conveniently avoided, and in general the rule of laissez-faire was afforded continued support, yet on specific matters both McCulloch and Senior supported an increase in government intervention. Examples may be found in relation to the regulation of buildings, public health measures, public transport, and even subsidising private industry in situations where a case could be made in the public interest.

The last great classical economist, John Stuart Mill also affirmed his belief in the rule of laissez-faire; as he stated in his *Principles*:

> Laissez-faire, in short, should be the general practice; every departure from it unless required by some great good will is certainly evil.[51]

Yet the actual departures from the rule which Mill so strongly advocated were in reality greater than those of any of his predecessors. He has indeed been referred to as:

> a transitional figure in the shift from a laissez-faire to an interventionist government.[52]

Book V of his *Principles, On the Influence of Government* is in fact concerned entirely with the question of the extent to which government intervention in the economic system is warranted. Therefore, while continuing to accept the framework of a contemporary classical political economy, he saw several arguments for intervention by the state. The deficiencies of the capitalist system which had manifest themselves over the preceding decades were no doubt a significant influence on his thinking.

Indeed, in later editions of the *Principles* and in his later life, Mill even expressed considerable sympathy for the concept of socialism. However to classify him as a socialist, especially a utopian socialist as does Heilbroner, would not be an accurate assessment. Some of his strongest pro-socialist statements are in fact little more than a statement of an ultimately desirable goal; his view in Robbin's words:

---

51 J. M. Robson (ed.): *Principles of Political Economy*, Book V, University of Toronto Press, 1965. p. 945.
52 R. Ramano and L. Leiman: Op Cit. p. 95.

related to an essentially vague ascent via co-partnership to some kind of co-operative productive association more syndicationalist than socialist in conception.[53]

One particular advance concluded by Mill was to suggest that as the processes of the production of goods and services are governed by certain laws, there are no such laws governing the distribution of wealth. In other words he established that the way the fruits of productive activity are distributed among the members of the community could be pre-determined, and in fact altered, by decisions made by that community. Obviously this opens the way for considerable potential for government intervention to achieve certain ends, particularly a more equitable distribution of the fruits of technical progress. For Mill recognised that it was:

> questionable if all mechanical inventions yet made have lightened the day's toil of any human being. They have enabled a greater population to live the same life of drudgery and imprisonment, and have increased the number of manufacturers and others to make fortunes.[54]

However, he also concedes that there were a number of exceptions to the rule of laissez-faire, especially regarding production and it is important to summarise the main arguments adduced by Mill in this regard. Initially it was concluded that the consumer may not be a competent judge of a particular commodity. This applied specifically to goods:

> the net worth of which demand of the market is by no means a test; things of which the utility does not consist in ministering to inclination, nor in serving the daily uses of life, and the want of which is least felt where the need is greatest.[55]

The provision of education is another prime example. In this regard Mill argued that no government should have a monopoly on the

53 L. Robbins: Op Cit. p. 116.
54 Ibid, p. 77.
55 J. M. Robson: Op Cit. p. 947.

provision of education. However he also conceded that this constituted an area where market forces alone would not provide education in a socially desirable or adequate fashion.

Further, the consumer might not, in some instances, be an adequate judge of his own interests. As an example, Mill discussed the inadequacies of individual management in cases where individuals could only manage the concern by delegated agency. This was a reference to joint stock companies which Mill thought were little different to a public authority and whose activities could just as well be performed by the government, or at the very least controlled by it.

In addition, in some specific cases, the government might be required, not to overrule the judgment of individuals respecting their own interest, but to give effect to that judgment. For example with respect to hours of labour it would be in the general interest of the working class to have hours of labour restricted to a predetermined number; yet it could also be argued that it might be in the immediate interests of individuals, in obtaining employment, to offer additional labour. It would therefore be in all individuals' interests to have the hours of work fixed by law.

Finally, it is established that some acts benefit the socioeconomic group generally as well as those undertaking them specifically. This illustrates very clearly the genesis of the theory of externalities. For example, as Mill explained, while a voyage of geographical or scientific exploration undertaken by private subscription might be of great public value, the expenses should more appropriately be borne by government. Similarly Mill regarded it as the proper office of government, to build and maintain public facilities, with proportional propensities to benefit specific segments of the socioeconomic group directly as well as to enhance the overall benefits through items of essentially social as well as private benefit. The question of the maintenance of a learned class may be regarded as a case in point.

Therefore while avoiding the temptation to reduce the works of the classical political economists in a generic sense, we may thus conclude that at least with respect to the issue we are most concerned with, namely the establishment of an appropriate political economic system, the specific contributions of the classical economists were significant. The famous Cambridge economist Alfred Marshall was to describe this period, at the end of the century, as the system of economic freedom. Lord Robins has summarised the classical position thus:

> Given a certain framework of law and order and certain necessary governmental services ... they (the classical political economist) conceived that the object of economic activity was best obtained by a system of spontaneous co-operation. As consumers, the citizens should be free to buy what best pleased their fancy. As producers, as workers or as owners and organisers of the means of production, they should be free to use their labour or their property in ways in which, in their judgment, would bring them the maximum reward in money or satisfaction. It is the impersonal mechanism of the market which, on this view brings it about that the interests of the different individuals are harmonised. To use Adam Smith's famous phrase, the individual seeking to direct industry that its produce may be of the greatest value "intends only his own gain", but "he is in this, as in many other cases, led by an invisible hand to promote an end which was no part of his intention". It follows that it should be a prime objective of policy that trade and commerce should be free, and that where obstacles to this spontaneous co-operation exist, they should be swept away.[56]

With respect to the issue of economic freedom, it is considered that it is established upon the notion that the political economy was based on certain pre-determined natural laws, and that the subsequent attempts to discern these laws were the inherent duties of the incipient economist; although as noted above, the notion started to break down with Mill's distinction between the laws of nature and those that may be considered merely customary. The general conclusion was that if these laws were left to function, without exogenous influences, then the wealth of nations would be maximised.

56 L. Robbins: Op Cit. p. 11.

However, it is essential to emphasise that this is quite a different proposition to suggesting that the conclusions of the classical economists were based on any notion of a Harmonielehre, that is to say the idea that there was some innate divine harmony in the social order. This interpretation essentially followed from a series of scientific conclusions based on certain assumptions about human nature, particularly that man was rational and self-interested. Given this understanding it was then reasonable to conclude that the force of the market was the most effective means of maximising human welfare. Clearly this then implies that the subsequent train of logic had to include a positive perception of the state. Market forces were not seen to create some sort of harmony in vacuo, but had to be strictly controlled; however the state was required to establish the functional parameters of the system.

Thus while the central contention may give strong inference to the premise that the market should be left to function in isolation within the political economy, the classical economists conceded that there were instances where this general rule should be invalidated. This was justified in the event that the socioeconomic circumstances warranted such action, from a subscription to the necessity of the social good. This subsequent concession to economic reality indicates that the classical economists were all, in different ways, men of affairs, prepared to prescribe the policies required to meet particular economic situations.

A J Taylor has suggested that it is necessary to distinguish between the analytical and the prescriptive elements in the classical economists' work. The prescriptions of the economists stand in relation to their analyses as politics is related to political theory. Politics, the art of the possible, must take account of factors and forces outside and additional to those which constitute the data on which the theoretician builds his ideal state, and likewise economic theory, when related to the situations of the common life, must accept the tempering influence of extra-economic forces.[57]

---

57 A. J. Taylor: *Laissez-Faire and State Intervention in Nineteenth Century Britain.* p. 25.

5

The Decline in Market Capitalism

The beginning of the decline, in practical application, of the theory of market capitalism, is seen as the end of an era in political economic development. It brings to a conclusion the examination of theoretical political economic concatenation to approximately 1870, and embodies the ascendancy of the market economy and the subsequent development and legitimisation of capitalism as an economic system. This process has also facilitated an insight into the sequence of hypothetical conceptions concerning the operation of the economic structure, and the extent to which it was conceded that economic activity ought, or ought not, to be controlled by the state.

As it may be deduced from preceding chapters, the critical developments in political economic theory, associated with the decline in market capitalism, are intimately related to the structure of industry and the role of the state in economic activity. It is also possible to interpret this as a concentration of private economic power. The essential focus of consideration in this context is the structure of the industrial base. As has been previously explained, within the parameters of a market economy, economic activity is undertaken in a variety of markets, specifically product markets and factor markets. Each market represents a meeting point facilitating transactions between all buyers and sellers of the particular product inherent within the same market, albeit a good, a service, or a factor of production.

The interaction of buyers and sellers in each market determines the quantity of the product or factor produced or traded, and the value at which it is transacted. The term market then, refers to the characteristics of the industry; one of which, and perhaps the most important in determining how the industry will function is the number of sellers, or firms, producing and selling the particular product. From the closing decades of the nineteenth century the structure of industries within capitalist systems underwent fundamental structural changes within this framework, and as such, this fundamentally altered the nature of the system, and the attendant macroeconomic theory required to interpret it.

In preceding chapters, mention has been made of the unparalleled consequences of the industrial revolution. However, the incidence of the significant number of industrial technical innovations created during the late eighteenth century, which marked the ascent of the revolution, was not the simple conclusion of an isolated historical event. Rather it was the inception of a process of technological change which has continued to accelerate, arguably to the present day.

Initially the industrial revolution was based mainly on textiles, on improvements in textile machinery and steam power. However, the second phase of industrialisation, did not materialise until around 1840. It was based, rather more securely, on coal, iron, steel, capital industries and above all the railway.

In both of these phases of industrialisation, the major focus of attention was to remain on Britain, however conveniently for the purposes of theoretical comparison, both Britain and American largely conformed to the theoretical model of perfect competition. That is, by definition if not practice, industries comprised of a large number of relatively small firms producing a fairly standardised product. The market thus worked, in these industries, in much the same way that Adam Smith described in *The Wealth of Nations*.

However, the third and most profound industrial revolution occurred in about 1870, where the most substantial innovation was the role of science and technology. Developments in chemistry, in the ability to generate electrical power and the invention and refinement of the internal combustion engine were the basis of a coherent range of industries based on scientific technology. Additionally, it was in this phase of industrial development that America was to demonstrate a capacity for more industrial dynamism than Britain.

One of the major consequences of the technological revolution was the introduction into the production process of mass production. A prominent structural feature of this event was that it yielded what may be regarded today as economies of scale. That is to say, the larger the scale of operations, the lower the subsequent unit cost of producing the product, to the point of production apathy. It obviously followed that, for the individual firm, there were advantages to be gained from size. The result was a process of inevitable concentration of production and ownership within industries. Hobsbawm expresses this as:

> The rise of an economy composed of a handful of great lumps of rock-trusts, monopolies, oligopolies rather than a large number of pebbles.[58]

The techniques of large-scale production, arising out of advances in scientific technology, thus created a situation which threatened to alter the integral definition of competition. Adam Smith interpreted competition to be a mechanism that prevented any single firm from dominating the market; however in this case it was clearly conducive to creating a situation where an ever larger share of the market was dominated by the largest and most efficient producers, a situation clearly contemplated with distaste by Smith.

The process of concentration became most clearly visible in America and Germany as early as the 1880s. In 1888 a law was passed in New Jersey allowing a corporation chartered in the state to buy stock in another corporation. The way was therefore open for the corporate merger. Over the next several decades there were numerous examples of mergers as a result of this facility, so that inevitably the way was paved for a number of small companies to merge into industrial conglomerations.

This phenomenon, combined with the rapid internal growth of the number of corporations, resulted in the process of concentration, described above, in the industrial structure of nearly all manufacturing industries. The first comprehensive study of this process was one

---

58   E. Hobsbawm: *Industry and Empire*, Pelican, 1969. p. 177.

undertaken by Adolf Berie and Gardiner Means in the early 1930s. They saw it as process whereby:

> a society in which production is carried on under the ultimate control of a handful of individuals.[59]

Looking into the future, Berie and Means concluded:

> Just what does this rapid growth of big companies promise for the future? Let us project the trend of the growth of recent years. If the wealth of the large corporations and that of all corporations should each continue to increase for the next twenty years from 1909 to 1929, 70 percent of all corporate activity would be carried on by two hundred corporations in 1950. If the more rapid rates of growth from 1924 to 1929 were maintained for the next twenty years 85 percent of corporate wealth would be held by two hundred huge units. If the indicated growth of the large corporations and of the national wealth were to be effective from now until 1950, half of the national wealth would be under the control of big companies at the end of the period.[60]

In Britain the process of concentration proceeded much more slowly. Indeed the closing years of the nineteenth century have been described by Hobsbawm as:

> a sudden transformation of the leading and most dynamic industrial economy into the most sluggish and conservative.[61]

Why this was so is one of the most intriguing questions of British economic history; it is a question which goes beyond the scope of this investigation. However, we may benefit from an introduction to one aspect of this decline in industrial prestige, in that contrary to the American experience, and to some learned opinions in academic and business circles of what was considered desirable, industry in

59 R. L. Heiibroner: *The Making of Economic Society*, Fourth Edition, Prentice-Hall, 1972. p. 123.
60 Ibid, p. 120.
61 E. Hobsbawm; Op Cit. p. 178.

Britain remained relatively unconcentrated while industry in America was undergoing the process described above.

This was particularly evident up until 1914. Despite a number of important mergers and monopolistic arrangements which were concluded around the turn of the century, the British industrial structure continued to be dominated by a multiplicity of small, independent and highly individualistic business units right up to the First World War. The situation changed considerably after the war; in fact the war itself, during which competition was suppressed in the national interest, gave considerable impetus to change.

At the end of this period, a committee which was appointed to consider the appropriate post-war commercial and industrial policy, pointed out that the replacement of competition with co-operation and the amalgamation of firms, was a reality, was inevitable under modern conditions, and that it was moreover desirable. The period following the First World War was for the British, contrary to America, characterised by depressed economic conditions. This was principally due to the fact that the old staple industries such as coal, shipbuilding, iron, steel and cotton, on which much of Britain's nineteenth-century superiority had rested, maintained their inefficient competitive structures. Furthermore these industries were not able to regain markets lost during the war.

Within the British context, the new post-war industries such as motor vehicles, chemicals and electrical products failed to develop sufficiently to replace the old staple industries. There were, however, serious attempts at what was generally termed rationalisation of British industry in the inter-war years. Rationalisation was defined as:

> industrial combination not to secure monopolistic advantages but to secure economics of production and distribution of a process necessary to produce higher organisation rather than to confer monopolistic advantages.

For the purpose of this investigation, the details of this process are not important; it is sufficient to note that there was, in most of the major industries in Britain, a rapid and marked process of concentration in industry. Hobsbawm has in fact suggested that:

> in 1914 Britain was perhaps the least concentrated of the great industrial economies, and in 1939 one of the most.[62]

It is also worthy of note in view of our understanding of classical political economic theory, that the process was encouraged by the state. Indeed in some cases the state played a major initiating role, after meeting with marked resistance from entrepreneurs. This contrasted substantially with the experience in America.

The second major change in capitalism, as the principal focus of an economic system concerned the role of government in economic activity; the first, relating to the structure of private industry. Previously the 1850s and 1860s in Britain were described as the decades where the doctrine of laissez-faire was established in practice in a relatively accurate form. However, it is clear that after 1870, the foundations of laissez-faire began to crumble. This collapse continued for the following four decades, culminating at the First World War. However, in contrast, some notable features such as the early factory legislation of the high years of laissez-faire were extended, consolidated and effectively enforced.

Yet inevitably a significant range of legislation affecting conditions of labour in general developed toward the end of the period. Legislation was initiated to restrict hours of work in 1908 and wages in 1914 in the coal mining industry. Trade boards were established to fix minimum wages and maximum hours in a group of sweated trades where labour was grossly exploited. Simultaneously there was a steady increase in government involvement with public goods and services, water, electrical, gas, transport, housing, education and public health.

In other words, not only was it recognised that in the process of production, in a free market system, certain evils were likely to arise to be inevitably combatted by legislation as described above; but also that certain desirable goods and services would either be

---

62 Ibid, p. 214.

produced inadequately or not at all. Even more notable were the measures taken during the period which were directed primarily towards altering the distribution of income and providing a greater degree of social security. Many of these were introduced by the last liberal governments in the years 1908–1914, though there were moves well before this. The introduction in 1908 of old-age pensions and in 1911 of unemployment and health insurance under the National Insurance Act in which Lloyd George and Chancellor of the Exchequer, Winston Churchill, were the prime movers, marked a significant increase in the political economic role of the state in a socioeconomic context.

However the extent of the changes to the system as a whole, that these policies implied must not be exaggerated. Many of them indeed were directed, more or less explicitly, at the maintenance of the capitalist system and at averting any direct challenge to it by those who saw some of its features as fundamentally unsatisfactory. The socialists, especially the Fabians, became increasingly active after the 1880s and in the words of one commentator:

provided the spectre of an ultimately socialist society which might eventuate if discontent with the existing order became excessive.[63]

The extent to which the new social policies of the time with which much of the increased government activity was concerned, were directed essentially towards undermining and heading off socialism, as it was fairly clear that Bismark in Germany was doing, is still a subject of much debate. It is significant too, that the citadel of free trade remained, at the start of the First World War, untouched after a decade of fairly concerted attack. Nevertheless, this period, represented a significant change in the system, to the point that it was eventually considered that a government could, and widely recognised that it should, interfere with the blind operation of market forces to improve the economic welfare of society as a whole.

---

63 D. Fraser: *Evolution of the British Welfare State*, Macmillan, 1973. p. 129.

The inter-war years in Britain were, as has already been noted, ones of generally depressed economic conditions, leading to the particularly difficult economic period of the early 1930s which came to be known as The Depression. This period saw little extension to the welfare schemes initiated before the war; rather, as part of the general attempt to cut government expenditure they were reduced in some respects. The major change in the government's involvement in economic life came, however, with increased intervention in industry. During the war, the government had exerted considerable control over a number of industries with remarkable effects on productivity. In Hobsbawm's words:

> between 1916 and 1918 Britain was forced to evolve a first incomplete and reluctant sketch of that powerful state economy of the Second World War.[64]

Controls were hastily dismantled immediately after the war, in line with the still prevailing ideology of economic liberalism; but when the extent of the difficulties most of the industries on which Britain's industrial economy depended became clear, there followed, during the 1920s and 1930s what Hobsbawm has termed:

> an unprecedented era of state intervention in business.[65]

This intervention was aimed principally at making private industry more efficient as distinct from replacing it, which is to say nationalising it. This meant breaking down the traditional competitive and dispersed pattern of private industry. In other words, it was the government which was behind the process of rationalisation discussed above, though the essential aim was to strengthen private business. As Hobsbawm states:

> Between the wars, and especially during the 1930s Britain turned from one of the least into one of the most trustified or controlled economies largely through direct government action. It achieved the amalgamation of the railways (1912), the

64 E. Hobsbawm: Op Cit. p. 240.
65 Ibid, p. 241.

concentration – indeed the partial nationalisation – of electricity supply (1926), the creation of a government sponsored monopoly in iron and steel (1932) and a national coal cartel (1936), though success was less in cotton. Equally unthinkable in terms of Victorian Capitalism, the government set about regulating prices and output by legal compulsion, notably in agriculture, about one third of whose output was brought into state-sponsored marketing schemes in the early thirties (pigs, bacon, milk, potatoes and hops). By the end of the 1930s some of these schemes had reached the verge of nationalisation – for example of coal royalties (1938) and of British airlines (1939) – while the collapse of industry in the depressed areas had produced at least the principle of a policy for the direct and subsidised fostering of industry by government planning.[66]

Perhaps the most radical change of all however, was the abandonment of free trade. Tariffs to protect Britain's ailing industries were introduced in 1931.

And since free trade was the almost religious symbol of the old competitive capitalist society, its end not merely demonstrated as it were publicly that a new era had begun, but encouraged the vast extension of government management. While it lasted, government action was an exception and an individual and regrettable departure from the ideal, which had to be carefully scrutinised and strictly limited. After it had gone, what was the point of measuring it in the homeopathic loses of the part?[67]

However, in contrast, the younger and more dynamic economy in America did not exhibit the same deficiencies as Britain and the necessity for government intervention was not seen in the same terms, at least until the catastrophe of the great depression. The major exception to this general statement specifically concerns international

66 Ibid, p. 242
67 Ibid, pp. 242–3.

trade. Protective tariffs were extensively employed throughout the period, and as such, were seen as a deliberate attempt at intervention by government to obstruct the operation of laissez-faire on behalf of domestic manufacturing interests.

The principles of economic liberalism and free enterprise were otherwise embraced and there was little other notable increase in government intervention during this period except, paradoxically perhaps, in attempts made after 1890 to ensure that the conditions under which the invisible hand of market competition was understood to work were maintained.

Economic theory and ideology suggested that under certain conditions, namely competitive markets and the absence of monopoly, market forces would dictate the best use of resources. However the development of trusts and the process of concentration and the growth of large business corporations, resulted in the phenomenon of monopoly and oligopoly, which obviously presented problems. Hence, starting with the Sherman Antitrust Act in 1890 American governments attempted to curb the process of concentration by legislating against it. These Acts amounted to the use of public economic power to curb private economic power. It involved a new concept of political economy in economic rationalisation, and one which was to continue to grow, though not uniformly.

The basic rationale of such legislation however, was the preservation of a system which was interpreted as working well without the requirement for government intervention, in order for it to constitute a productive force; but restrictive of the influences beyond that necessary to provide and preserve the framework for the system. By the middle 1930s therefore, laissez-faire as a policy was dead. However it is important to note that at this point there was one respect in which the government declined to intervene, and that is in the area of what is today termed macroeconomic management.

6

Neoclassical Economics

Neoclassical economics represents the inevitable transition from the concept of political economy to economics, and further illustrates the rationalisation of the traditional concept of microeconomics to represent a standardised development of the mainstream of theoretical economics and economic ideology that is familiar to contemporary observers.[68]

The critical period in the development of Neoclassical economics was the thirty year interval between 1870 and 1900. This period was enhanced by a number of major economic philosophers, however their ideas were in many cases developed independently and there is no convenient pattern to be interpreted. For the first time writers from countries other than Britain made major contributions. Important names are William Stanley Jevons and Alfred Marshall in Britain, Carl Menger in Austria, Leon Walras of the University of Lausanne and J B Clark in America.[69]

The period was one in which transpired what may be best described as an increasing professionalisation of economics. There was an attempt to concentrate on the discovery of purely scientific truths about the nature of economic activity and to discern objective economic laws. The extent to which this is possible and the extent to which the Neoclassical economists actually excluded ideology from their analysis is a matter of debate and is an issue which is still considered

68 L. G. Reynolds: *Economics. A General Introduction*, Richard D. Irwin, Inc., Homewood, Illinois. Third Edition. 1969. pp. 3–14.
69 W. H. Richmond: *Jevons, Sidgwick and Marshall on the Role of the State in Economic Activity.* University of Queensland, 1982. Inclusive.

contentious, however it is necessary to emphasise that the major developments in this period were in formal economic analysis.

These developments in analysis involved a considerable narrowing of focus. After 1850 the benefits of industrialisation were more apparent to the population generally, and there was a mood of optimism attributed to economic progress. The concerns of those who studied economics, therefore shifted from the larger, dynamic question of 'whither the system' or in contemporary terminology, 'economic growth' to the mechanics of the system. Adam Smith had provided a very general analysis of the market mechanism; the Neoclassicists now provided a full and precise working insight into the mechanism.

By far the greatest attention was afforded to what is now known as price theory. In doing this they maintained and formalised the Smithian concept of the egocentric and self maximising 'economic man', like the classical economists they also implicitly assumed that markets comprised large numbers of buyers and sellers or, again to use modern terminology, that there was pure competition.

However, they rejected the view that the determination of price or exchange-value could be explained solely from a cost standpoint, that is to say, by looking exclusively at the issue of production. The key concept of utility[70] entered the analysis, and value was now explained in terms of the marginal utility theory. This implied that the emphasis was placed on demand rather than supply, which constituted a direct threat to the traditional conception of Say's Law, which insisted that supply created demand, thus denying the evidence of under-consumption theories of a generalised lack of aggregate demand.

In Britain, the concept was first analysed by Jevons in his *Principles of Political Economy* published in 1870. Marginal utility or in Jevons terms 'the final degree of utility' was defined as the addition to total utility, or satisfaction, obtained from the last unit of a commodity purchased. It was further suggested that marginal utility decline as

---

70 F. R. Glahe and D. R. Lee: *Microeconomics, Theory and Applications*, Harcourt Brace and Jovanovich International Edition, New York, 1981. pp. 450–52.

more and more of a commodity was consumed, and was expressed as the 'law of diminished marginal utility.'

If consumers attempt to maximise their satisfaction or utility it then follows that consumers will allocate income such that marginal utility received from spending a dollar on any one commodity will be equal to the marginal utility received from spending one dollar on any other commodity. Hence a consumer will adjust his purchases of commodities so that the ratios of their marginal utilities will be equal to the ratios of their prices. The significance of this premise was that it solved what was termed as the paradox of value. Therefore in Jevons' view:

> the final degree of utility is that function upon which the theory of economics will be found to turn.

Marshall, who published his *Principles* twenty years later, considered that Jevons had given too much emphasis to utility. Rather, Marshall considered that both the cost of production and marginal utility principle should be combined, and on the basis of this view developed what is now the standard supply and demand analysis of introductory micro economics.[71] Price is determined where supply and demand forces are in equilibrium.

This is often referred to as the *Marshallian synthesis*. The Marshallian synthesis was an important step towards the understanding of the interdependence of all the elements of a market system. Marshall concentrated however, on what is now termed partial equilibrium analysis that is on the analysis of the determination of price in a particular market holding all other factors constant.

The extension of this analysis of the economic system to all markets, is attributed to Leon Walras. From his theories emerged general equilibrium analysis. Using a rigorous mathematical approach Walras showed that in a system of perfectly free competitive markets, for both products and the factors of production, demand and supply will

---

71 W. J. Barber: 'Alfred Marshall and the Framework of Neo-Classical Economics'. *A History of Economic Thought.* pp. 163–97.

always be brought into equilibrium at a price that will effect both consumer tastes, according to the utility derived and the costs of production.[72] This serves to illustrate the contention that even though the focus of economic analysis and the range of economic problems under consideration had narrowed, the period saw the development of the first truly comprehensive analysis of economic phenomena.

However not all of the interpretations of this aspect of Neoclassical economics were as enthused as the preceding examples. In his discussion of Neoclassical economics, Canterbery tends to play down the significance of the developments in the late nineteenth century. So far as their implications for ideology are concerned, he suggests they only reinforce the ideology of classical political economy, namely laissez-faire.

He claims that the Neoclassical revolution had all the excitement of a Sunday school picnic and refers to the Neoclassical economists, somewhat patronisingly, as;

> a group of clarifiers who examined the workings of the system in considerable detail but who expressed no fundamental doubts about its basic worth. Like the classical economists they believed that economic laws were natural laws that should not be tampered with.[73]

In other words Canterbery argues that the Neoclassicals were only doing, with a bit more precision, what the classical economists had done; to argue that a sort of natural harmony existed and that natural laws should be left free to operate. Other writers have made similar claims. Hunt and Sherman, for example, have suggested that:

> The Neoclassical economists gave a very elaborate and esoteric analytical defence of Adam Smith's notion of the invisible hand of market competition and the economic policy of laissez-faire.[74]

72 E. R. Weintraub and P. A. Samuelson: 'The Microfoundations of Macroeconomics; A Critical Survey', *Journal of Economic Literature*. March 1977, Volume XV, Number 1. p. 8.
73 J. M. Robson (ed.): Op Cit. p. 945.
74 E. K. Hunt and H. J. Sherman: *Economics: An Introduction to Traditional and Radical Views*, Harper and Row, 1972. pp. 97–98.

It is considered that Canterbery has over emphasised and simplified the concept of natural harmony. He rests his argument, to a large extent, on the writings of J B Clark who was mainly concerned with factor markets and hence with the mechanism by which income was distributed in the market system; the essence of his argument was that the distribution of the income of society is controlled by a natural law, and that this law, if it worked without friction, would distribute to every agent of production the amount of wealth which the agent creates. The clear implication was that the mechanism should be allowed to work without friction. However it is necessary to emphasise that the views of Clark were not typical.

Nevertheless the Neoclassicals did talk about law. It is also true that the new and more precise analysis of these laws were used to draw the conclusion, and state it in much more precise terms, that a free competitive market system was in a specific sense an ideal type; this had first been demonstrated by Walras in what he termed the 'doctrine of maximum satisfactions' and was stated in its most refined form by the Italian economist Vilfredo Pareto. Pareto emphasised that given the distribution of income, a free and competitive market would ensure the maximisation of the total utility of the consumer system.[75]

Largely for this reason the Neoclassicals accepted what was generally termed the 'rule of laissez-faire'. It is not the case however, that they were extreme advocates of a system of laissez-faire. Canterbery does concede that Marshall, for example,

> had a greater flexibility towards laissez-faire economics than many of his classical predecessors.

However, he generally gives too little credit to the Neoclassicists' recognition that, despite the doctrine of maximum satisfaction, there were many shortcomings of a free market system, and that government

---

75 P. A. Samuelson: 'Strengths of a Mixed Economy', in *Economic Impact*, Number 36, 1981/4. pp. 26–8.

intervention with economic laws was in many cases justified. Some brief comments about the views of major British Neoclassical economists will illustrate the point.

Jevons, for example opened his inaugural lecture in 1876 with an affirmation of faith in the value of free internal and external commerce and a lament that the centenary of the publication of the book in which these principles were first stated, *The Wealth of Nations* was not being duly celebrated. However it closed with a suggestion that even though,

> the laissez-faire principle properly applied is the wholesome and true one the extension of government activity may be warranted in a number of cases.[76]

Jevons' proposals, in his various writings, for increased government action related almost entirely to those cases where market forces were inadequate to efficiently provide goods or services which people wanted or needed, that is cases of inadequacies of individual choice. Such inadequacies were seen by Jevons to be due largely to ignorance on the part of consumers, the public nature of certain goods and services, and also externalities or the neighbourhood effect, and they often contained an element of paternalism.

He argued for public rather than the private operation of telegraph services, and for a state parcel post. He advocated a role for the Government with respect to slum clearance, public housing, the provision of museums, public libraries, concerts, art galleries, parks and halls; arguing that market forces alone would not ensure a socially desirable production of these goods and services, at least to poorer people. In his final book, *The State in Relation to Labour* Jevons recognised that the terms of the relationships between capital and labour needed to be increasingly controlled by the government. All these activities of the state are accepted without question today, however, a century ago these were matters of significant contention. There is an obvious tendency to interpret this as fairly weak

---

76 W. H. Richmond: Op Cit. Inclusive.

bourgeoisie reformism, while to some, such proposals were a challenge to fundamental political economic principles.[77]

Alfred Marshall also offered an opinion of this contentious issue, and while his views did not differ fundamentally from those of Jevons, they were presented more comprehensively. It would be appropriate to label Marshall as an individualist, rather than a socialist. He once said:

> Progress depends very much on our getting the right men into the right places, and giving them a free hand and sufficient inducement to exert themselves to the utmost.

He associated ingenuity, initiative and creativity with private enterprise and used terms like 'the iron fist of socialism' and 'the dead hand of bureaucracy' to describe the alternative.

> A government could print a good edition of Shakespeare's works, but it could not get them written. The carcass of municipal electric works belongs to free enterprise.[78]

Yet in many of his writings Marshall advocated greater government intervention in economic activity on issues such as education, housing and, in an anticipatory way, the environment. He also thought that the increasing elements of private monopoly, which he considered likely to occur following the very marked trends in this regard in America, needed to be controlled by governments. With respect to distribution, he declared existing inequalities of wealth to be a 'serious flaw in our economic organisation' and approved of progressive rates of income tax and a moderate increase in death duties.

Therefore, at the same time as economists were affording more credibility to the investigation of the theory of the market mechanism, and demonstrating how it may be generally employed to maximise economic welfare, given the distribution of income, they were increasingly conceding deficiencies in the laissez-faire principle and

---

77 Ibid.
78 W. J. Barber. Op Cit. pp. 163–97.

advocating that the market mechanism should be interfered with or overridden in certain instances to secure socially desirable results. However, it is relevant to ensure that the significance of these views is not over-emphasised, as it was advocated, in nearly all cases in response to actual events.

It would seem reasonable to conclude at this juncture that the Neoclassical economists did not generally advocate any government action that was not already being pursued, or at least debated, in the more practical arena of politics; indeed there were some such actions they continued to reject. Moreover the deficiencies recognised were those normally associated with a purely competitive market system; problems of providing public goods, externalities, securing an equitable distribution of income etc.

Clearly the analysis of the Neoclassical economists of the late nineteenth century was overwhelmingly in reference to free competitive markets, in which it was assumed, implicitly or explicitly, that there were a large number of buyers and sellers; in the case of product markets this meant, more specifically, that there were a large number of small firms, none of which had any control over the operation of the market.

Monopoly was discussed, but only the case of pure monopoly, one firm, was incorporated into the theory, notably by Marshall. Yet one of the most significant changes that took place in the capitalist system in the late nineteenth and early twentieth centuries was the process of concentration.[79] Obviously markets were ceasing to be purely competitive, yet they were not monopolistic in a pure sense either. Clearly the general rule to which the Neoclassicists still held was therefore increasingly based on a fairly large chasm between economic theory and economic reality.

79 T. J. Hailstones: *Economics, An Analysis of Principles and Policies*, Second Edition, South-West Publishing Company, Brighton, 1975. p. 650.

7

The Keynesian Revolution

When undertaking an examination of economic theory it is evident that it is possible to divide the investigation into two categories, that is macroeconomic and microeconomic theory. From this perspective it is also possible to take macroeconomic theory and further divide it into Classical and Keynesian theory. However, there is an all-important difference between these divisions, for whereas macro and micro theory are strictly additive, classical and Keynesian theory are largely alternative.

Additionally, macro and micro theory are accepted as parts of a total, however Keynesian theory is accepted only by rejecting parts of Classical theory. It is considered inappropriate to argue the relative merits of macro and micro theory, for they are largely noncompetitive branches of theory, both of which are necessary to a complete theory of the economy. However the relative merits of Classical and Keynesian theory of the economy are extensively debated for their basic postulates and conclusions are opposed.

It is necessary to point out that it is impossible to underestimate the importance of the Keynesian impact on contemporary macroeconomic theory, however it is equally essential to define the exact meaning of Keynesian macroeconomic theory. Here Keynes himself may be singled out as the founding authority. However his role is restricted to this, as it is necessary to make a distinction between 'the economics of John Maynard Keynes' and 'Keynesian economics'. The economics of Keynes, primarily his *General Theory* is the foundation on which Keynesian economics has been constructed. Following the publication of this book, economists went through it line by line, accepting, correcting, and rejecting. What they have built on the foundation that remained is a massive economic structure known as Keynesian economics.[80]

It is also important to ensure that not only is there a clear distinction between Classical theory and Keynesian theory, but it is also necessary to identify the context of what is merely an extension of Classical ideas that were not spelled out by the Classical economists. This enables an appreciation to be established of what was clearly wrong in Classical theory, at least in relation to the urbanised and industrialised economy of the twentieth century. These are extremely complex issues that economists continue to debate. Still, the significance of what was advanced as new in the economics of Keynes or 'new economics', as measured by its widespread acceptance, has few equals in the history of economic doctrine.[81]

The widespread acceptance of large parts of Keynesian economics over the past quarter-century has necessarily been equated with the widespread rejection of large parts of Neoclassical macroeconomics. Acceptance of a theory that showed that an economy may be in equilibrium with less than full employment amounted to a rejection of parts of Neoclassical theory that maintained that the only equilibrium position was the limited theoretical state of full employment. This is the most fundamental of the differences in the conclusions reached by the two theories, and may be expressed as:

$$F(N,K) = C(f(N,K);\emptyset) + I(q) + G, C'(Y) < 1, 1'(q) > 0$$

Where consumption expenditures, C is made to depend upon income according to the usual consumption function, and upon a

---

80 In more recent years several economists have argued that this structure in certain fundamentals involves some misinterpreting of what Keynes really said. From this point of view, Keynesian economics differs from the economics of Keynes in part in its failure to correctly grasp the meaning of Keynes' words. This is a major theme of the book *On Keynesian Economics and the Economics of Keynes* (Oxford University Press, 1968), by A. Leijonhufvud. See also R. W. Clower, 'The Keynesian Counterrevolution; A Theoretical Appraisal', in F. H. Hahn and F. P. R. Brechling, editors, *The Theory of Interest Rates*, Macmillan, 1965.

81 It is interesting that the success of Keynes was perhaps equalled by that of Ricardo, whose economics Keynes attacked. As Keynes put it, 'Ricardo conquered England as completely as the Holy Inquisition conquered Spain', *The General Theory*, p. 3.

shift parameter ø. Investment expenditure, I is an increasing function of q once the latter is high enough to induce positive gross investment. Government expenditure, is taken to be exogenous, and the supply price is represented in terms of q, of the investment implied by a given N, that is, the value of q needed to induce that level of investment and associated level of employment.

Additionally, q and N invert the demand for real cash balances and function to obtain the wealth owners required money rate of interest, i, as a function of, I of income and real cash balances. This implies that the expected nominal rate of return on shares where the latter is the expected inflation rate, which is a function of the level of employment, denoted as h(N), plus the expected rate of change and return on shares expressed in terms of q. As M denotes the money supply, W the money wage level, and taking the price level to be marginal cost, hence equal to W/FN (K, N), where FN is the marginal product of labour, it is possible to express this as:

$$I\left\{F(K,N), Mo/[Wo/FN(K,N)]\right\} = (1/q)[FK(K,N) - O + qe]$$
$$+ h(N), I1\, FN + I2\,(M/W)\, FNN > (1/q)\, FKN + h'$$

The practical significance and the implications of what lies behind this development cannot be over emphasised as a critical development in political economic theory, as it relates to political economic theory. In directing his attack at the Neoclassical concept of an economic system equilibrating at full employment and presenting a general theory of under-employment equilibrium, of which the Neoclassical theory was a special case, Keynes' polemical instinct was considered to be very attractive. This is due to the fact that Neoclassical interpretations were seen to be a major obstacle to the implementation of anti-depression policies and because, for professional economists, the concept of equilibrium has always had far more intellectual appeal as an analytical companion than its opposite, disequilibrium.

Obviously if the Keynesian argument is accepted, that left on its own the economy may not move toward or attain the position of full employment, the argument must accept the use of policies, designed to achieve this objective, that were discounted by the quite different arguments of Neoclassical theory. It is considered that the ultimate purpose of any economic theory is to establish a contribution for a sound basis for political economic policy actions, and the subsequent widespread acceptance of Keynesian theory over the past two decades, has increasingly led to the adoption of some policies suggested by that theory.

As many economists are fond of pointing out, the massive US federal tax cut of 1964 amounted to an acceptance of Keynesian theory by the US Congress. This constituted a legitimisation of fiscal responsibility where the key policy weapon for stimulating the economy towards full employment could assume the form of increased government spending or tax cuts, or both. Indeed, monetary policy was held to be of small, or even trivial, importance as a tool for the influence of aggregate demand. However, to obtain any real understanding of the rationale for this and other policy actions, one must first gain an understanding of the essence of Keynesian theory. It is necessary to interpret his work as a fundamental attack on a body of theory that he designated Classical theory. The major concepts outlined by Keynes are to be found in his article 'The General Theory of Employment', in the quarterly *Journal of Economics* (1939), which was an article written in response to various critics, concisely restating the arguments of *The General Theory of Employment, Interest and Money* (1936).[82] In the General Theory itself, the major emphasis is considered to be found in 'The State of Long Term Expectations', and in 'The Essential Properties of Interest and Money', both of which have their provenance in *The End of Laissez-Faire* (1926), published some ten years earlier.[83]

It is essential to emphasise at this juncture that this paradigm must be interpreted within the context of the parameters that Keynes considered as central to the economic analysis, against those he considered merely peripheral; and in view of elements essential to the investigation as opposed those that were clearly incidental. Thus by

82 J. M. Keynes: *The General Theory of Employment Interest and Money*, Macmillan, 1936.
83 J. M. Keynes: *The End of Laissez-Faire*, London, Macmillan, 1936.

calling attention to the inherent weaknesses in the Neoclassical system, or at least a recognisable caricature of it, Keynes also called into question the method of analysis by which the system was constructed.

Keynes chose to emphasise the relevance of Neoclassical theory with realistic application, where it was demonstrated that the only practical example of the theory applied to the unique case of equilibrium, where expectations were assumed in an empirical form.[84] Risks were allocated as identifiable criteria but little attention was afforded them, and uncertainty was reduced to the same calculable status as certainty.[85] Keynes claimed that the absence of any technique for dynamic analysis resulted in an inability to deal with uncertainty in the economic future, by assuming the possession of knowledge of the future in a calculable basis.

This was seen as a false rationalisation and misleading if applied to the economy at any position other than at equilibrium, which was a more realistic interpretation of economic reality.[86] His treatment of expectations in terms of 'states of expectations', and especially his distinction between short-period and long-period expectations, incorporated the pseudo-dynamics of the Marshallian distinction between short-period and long-period analysis.

The natural tendency in Classical reductionist theory is therefore to gravitate towards market equilibrium, as the choice-logic theory is relatively straight forward. This obviously highlights a weakness in the fundamental expression of the economy as there is no consideration of a natural gap between market demand and market supply, as each of these schedules is derived from an allegedly reasonable choice-logic theoretical structure.

However, Keynes countered this by emphasising that it was not possible to ignore the consequences of economic risk and

84 J. M. Keynes: Op Cit. p. 3.
85 J. M. Keynes: 'The General Theory of Employment', *Quarterly Journal of Economics*, February, 1937.
86 H. G. Johnson: 'The General Theory After Twenty-Five Years', *American Economic Review*, May, 1961. p. 2.

uncertainty[87] by describing them as calculable factors of an equilibrium economy, as by definition the future is uncertain and therefore
strictly rational behaviour is impossible.

Keynes was able to construct an argument for liquidity preference
which had devastating consequences for reductionist price theory
once applied to all assets. Once all prices are considered money
prices, and all assets incorporate a liquidity premium, price theory
is subject to expectational and conventional elements that characterise
Keynes' theory of the rate of interest. However Keynes' innovation in
analytical procedure by dealing with the rate of interest in association
with money-holding decisions, rather than with borrowing and lending,
should not be confused with his substantive contributions.

By concentrating on the irreducibly creative element in human
choice, where the concerns of expectations, uncertainty and ignorance,
which can be construed as knowledge surrogates in the face of a
knowledge deficiency, it is possible to construct an economic alternative to the classical concept of an economic system equilibrating
at full employment. Thus, it can be seen that the clearly specified
and stable objectives required by reductionist theory, are in fact
regarded by Keynes in the context of the actual basis of choice lying
in vague, uncertain and shifting expectations of future events and
circumstances. Keynes focused on the conventional elements in valuation, but insisted that they be rendered sustainable in the face of
minor events and of changes in circumstances.

This premise legitimises the concept of an economy on the basis of
accepted convention, thus establishing an embryonic macroeconomic
theory in distinct contrast to the acceptable convention of macroeconomics. The essential point is that once the choice theoretical foundations are threatened, the whole reductionist program is called into
question; for without them the market theory would have no basis
for foundation and no potential for education. Therefore with an
absence of any clearly specified and stable basis in choice-logic, the
idea of market equilibrium is no longer connected to the realisable.

---

87   J. Robinson: *The Generalisation of the General Theory*, St Martin's Press, New York, 1979. p. 59.

What this means is that the sustainability of equilibrium must depend on conditions that are confined to the level of the market.

Keynes' concepts obviously require the rethinking and reconstruction of the whole body of reductionist theory, its choice theoretical basis and the equilibrium theory of markets that rest on it. Keynes went further to point out that the Neoclassical case applied specifically to the special case of equilibrium where expectations were assumed to be given a definite and calculable form. Risks were identified, but little attention was afforded them, as certainty.

Keynes claimed that the lack of any technique for dynamic analysis resulted in an avoidance of the issues of uncertainty in the economic future, while assuming to possess a knowledge of the future in a calculable basis. For Keynes this was false rationalisation and misleading if applied to the economy at any position not in equilibrium, and thus detrimental to the ultimate progress of the economy, especially in anti-depression policy where the solution to a depression was to stimulate aggregate demand, given that the control of aggregate demand was an ultimate responsibility of public policy makers.[88]

Uncertainty and expectations within the economy are essential to the Keynesian paradigm, as fears and hopes of individuals have a significant influence on human behaviour; just as doubt, precautions, vague fears and unreasonable hopes create disillusionment and thus a new basis for valuation.[89] The emphasis concerning the uncertainty of the future, and the importance of opinions about the future are therefore interpreted as the fundamental motivation for action by business and consumers alike. It is considered that this emphasis may represent the most important innovation in the General Theory, however it is also evident that the significance of this revolutionary interpretation has been considerably underestimated.[90]

The essential relevance of economic uncertainty and expectations is best demonstrated by the relationship to the concept of time within

88 A. Murad: *What Keynes Means*, Bookman Associates, New York, 1962. p. 172.
89 J. M. Keynes: Op Cit.
90 D. Patinkin and J. C. Lefth: *Keynes, Cambridge and The General Theory*, The University of Ontario, 1977.

the economy and as such is associated with the theoretical concept
of the long-run and the short-run decisions and situations which have
short-run and long-run consequences.[91] However the Neoclassical
paradigm has no presupposed historical time or uncertainty concept,
and thus these decision making periods of activity, are not solely
influenced by fluctuations of market sales and prices, with no wrong
decisions, no mistakes, no uncertainty, and no disappointed expectations. History is seen as being irrelevant to economics, and time
is described as moving in two directions. Keynes concluded that
these assumptions about time and uncertainty are wrong, and obviously the implications for short-run uncertainty and expectations are
significant.[92]

For Keynes all economic activity takes place at a given place in
time, and thus decisions made in the past determine present actual
conditions of income, available capital stock, employment potential
etc.[93] The future is related to the present, by expectations, uncertainty
and contracts made in money terms. Thus each point in time has its
own particular past and own expectations of the future. All action
takes place now, which is the short-run, but the long-run occurs in
a future characterised by uncertainty and subject to expectations.

Therefore the concept of equilibrium has very little economic
relevance in view of Keynes analysis of value in physical terms, and
quantity is a measure based on labour and exchange occurring through
historical time.[94] The state of long-term expectations are considered
to be essential properties of interest rates, money and employment
levels as all prices are money prices and all assets bear a liquidity
premium, as price theory relies on expectations, as much as interest
rates. The implication is that:

91 V. Chick: *Inflation From A Longer Term Perspective: Lessons from the General Theory*,
University of London, 1983. p. 1.
92 V. Chick: *Macroeconomics After Keynes*. University of London. Philip Allan, 1983. p. 20.
93 V. Chick: 'The Nature of the Keynesian Revolution; A Reassessment', in *Australian Economic Papers*, Volume 17, June, 1978. p. 5.
94 A. Coddington: 'Keynesian Economics: A Search for First Principles', in *Journal of Economics*, Volume XIV, December, 1976. p. 1261.

expectations, uncertainty and ignorance are essentially knowledge surrogates in the face of a knowledge deficiency.[95]

Thus the Keynesian interpretation is a theoretical threat to the
foundation of reductionist market theory, which indicates that market
equilibrium is not logical, and the pursuit of this theory is an economic
distraction.[96] Keynes believed that the theoretical analysis of uncertainty and expectations not only provided a viable threat to the reductionist program, but also effectively introduced the economic
viability of disequilibrium trading by freeing economic theory from
irrelevant restrictions.

Keynes was therefore able to use his unique interpretation of
economic uncertainty and expectations to substantiate his belief in
the concept of the economy operating in disequilibrium, and this was
typified by the operation of disequilibrium trading.[97] If the concept
is accepted it can be seen that a polypolistic firm operating under
conditions of economic uncertainty, is not a price taker, as the fundamental feature of production is the allocation of community resources to production, for a market which exists in the future, and
is therefore uncertain.[98]

The essential implication formed from this interpretation of the
nature of the economy, is that the firm must form expectations of
the demand for its product, which is naturally a short-run expectation.[99] The expected position on the demand curve will essentially
determine the correct market price and the quantity required to satisfy
demand.

Obviously, the demand curve must be used because of the economic
uncertainty facing the firm, and it must incorporate the expectations
of the firm in relation to market demand and the supply of the
resources of other firms. From this illustration Keynes was able to

95   Ibid, p. 1260.
96   Ibid, p. 1263.
97   Ibid, p. 1270.
98   J. Eatwell: *Keynes's Economics and the Theory of Value and Distribution*, Duckworth, London,
1983. p. 12.
99   Ibid, p. 161.

shatter the myth of equilibrium as the only economically legitimate state of economic activity.[100]

The traditional Neoclassical interpretation of a firm where the price is determined by market forces and automatically represents demand, to the extent that there is no requirement to forecast demand, only to estimate output requirements, is therefore not realistic. If demand is presumed to be known and costs are predetermined on the basis of wages and technology levels, the equilibrium theory is admissible as an effective argument, however both conditions require the artificial assumption of perfect knowledge, which is not a tenable conclusion, given the existence of economic uncertainty and the requirements of expectations.

Therefore, the fundamental basis for the decisions of firms as to what output to produce, at what price, and therefore what quantity of labour to employ, is inevitably related to economic uncertainty.[101] Expectations determine what volume of output will produce the greatest profit, and profit expectations depend on the attendant costs, which determine in turn the amount of money at which firms are willing to sell output. This implies that according to Keynes' role of expectations, the volume of output at which firms decide to produce, depends on aggregate demand and aggregate supply. This is obviously in violation of the long standing traditions of Say's Law where supply is the factor that determines demand.[102] Additionally, there is a corresponding influence by expectations in an uncertain economy on the decision to invest money.

As with Say, pre-Keynesian economists tended to disregard the implications of expectations, and chose instead to determine the demand for capital according to past and present yields of capital equipment. Keynes however, rejected this view by indicating that it was a fundamental feature of a modern economy, and that it facilitated changing expectations concerning the future, to influence the volume

100   V. Chick: Op Cit. p. 22.
101   J. M. Keynes: *The General Theory and After, Part II Defence and Developments*, Macmillan, 1973. p. 113.
102   B. Seligman: *Main Currents in Modern Economics*, Quadrangle Books, Chicago, 1971. p. 735.

of investment and inevitably the quantity of employment and output.[103] Thus, having successfully rebutted the fundamental conceptions of the Neoclassical paradigm, within the economy, Keynes was able to conceptualise the existence of an economy functioning in disequilibrium with economic credibility. This enabled Keynes to specifically determine the relevance to employment, interest and money within the economy.

Given the existence of uncertainty concerning the future of economic events, there is a distinct incentive to hold money as a store of wealth.[104] Money may be used in this sense as a barometer of uncertainty and inherent distrust against future events and expectations. Therefore, the more cash an individual holds, the less is his level of insecurity and therefore, interest rates can be interpreted as an enticement to reduce cash holdings in the face of uncertainty.

Neoclassical theory claims that interest rates change because of the marginal efficiency of capital, however, this depends largely on the price of the capital asset, and this price determines the rate of new investment. However, Keynes claimed that this only occurred at the unique situation of equilibrium, where there was one rate of money income, and the marginal efficiency of capital was determined by a given money income rate. Keynes claimed that at disequilibrium there could be no tacit assumption of money income level, because all available resources were not employed, and as such the marginal efficiency of capital did not determine interest rates, but interest rates determined the marginal efficiency of capital.[105]

In reality Keynes pointed out that the marginal efficiency of capital was the expected rate of profit and thus determined the level of investment. Interest rates were a monetary phenomenon, subject to expectations and uncertainty, and the demand for and supply of money.[106] Perhaps Keynes should not have associated the marginal

103 V. Chick: Op Cit. p. 5.
104 B. Seligman: Op Cit. p. 736.
105 H. G. Johnson: Op Cit. p. 4.
106 J. R. Hicks: 'Mr Keynes and the Classics, A Suggested Interpretation', in *Econometrica*, Volume 5, 1937. p. 152.

efficiency of capital and interest rates, but the implications are obvious. Interest rates are the reward offered for parting with liquidity
for a period of time, as uncertainty within the economy changes the
demand for money, or liquidity preference, which in turn causes interest
rates to change.[107] Thus the liquidity preference affects changing interest
rates, and interest rates affect the total stock of cash. Uncertainty in
this process becomes the catalyst behind money manipulation.

Therefore, in conditions of economic uncertainty, when expectations are pessimistic, interest rates will decline as there is less incentive to decrease money holdings, and an increased desire to hold
cash, while in conditions of optimism interest rates will increase as
there is less desire to hold cash.[108] Investment is further affected in
this fashion as decreasing interest rates cause an increase in preference
for capital assets such as bonds. Thus any decrease in interest rates
usually means an increase in the price of bonds, while an increase
in interest rates results in a decrease in the price of bonds.

As a result, uncertainty sets the economic climate and expectations
determine the actions appropriate to the situation as a gamble on un-
certainties between cash and securities. The unique feature of this system
is that if enough people believe the money market will rise or fall, it
eventually will. This implies that any substantial expectations concerning
the future of interest rates, will create a subsequent change in interest
rates.[109] The investor is then forced to assume that the existing economic
state will continue, unless there exists a significant belief that a change
will alter this. There is a requirement to rely on the maintenance of
conventions, to enable the investor to believe in his own judgment and
the security of his investment over short-term periods of expectations.

It is evident that real and monetary phenomena are enjoined in an
economy characterised by uncertainty over the possible outcomes
and future events, that is, a monetary economy.[110] Additionally there

---

107   J. Robinson: Op Cit. p. 142.
108   Ibid, p. 20.
109   V. Chick: Op Cit. p. 5.
110   J. M. Keynes: *On the Theory of a Monetary Economy*, Duncker and Humbolt, Munich, 1933.
p. 123.

are further implications for the relationship between savings and investment to further affect the general price level, as Keynes points out that the interrelationship between monetary and real variables in the face of uncertainty, affects levels of savings and investment through aggregate demand and employment, which are secondary considerations.

Keynes therefore, offered a short period theory of effective demand, and the interrelations of a monetary system which invalidated Say's Law and the Quantity Theory of Money and this differentiates Keynes' system from the real-barter exchange economy. This is the initial step into Keynes' theory of employment and short-term, long-term output analysis. Money is not afforded a principal role in the analysis, as monetary relations are essentially related to equilibrium economic conditions.

The main emphasis Keynes placed on money is related to the fact that the future is uncertain and unpredictable, and thus money provides the most certain insurance against an uncertain future, as it is the most liquid and least risky asset as a store of value over time.[111] Interest earning assets would be preferred to cash if there was no doubt as to their future value, because interest rates are the price for finance and the rate of profit expected on investment is the marginal efficiency of capital.

This means that there is no equilibrium value of money, or price level as the value of money is determined by the level of money wages at any moment in time, thus creating the necessity for rigid money wages to ensure that the value of money does not alter rapidly and lose credibility against an uncertain future. Wages are paid in terms of a value which is determined by the overall operation of the economy, and not a single market.

Thus, unemployment in Keynesian terms, is due to a maladjustment of money wage rates against the money supply.[112] Investment and liquidity are not seen as relevant, as employment relates to a demand for output, rather than real wages. Disturbances such as these, lower the marginal efficiency of capital, and increase the supply of

111 J. Eatwell: Op Cit. p. 251.
112 A. Leijonhufvud: 'Keynes and the Classics', in *The Institute of Economic Affairs* – Occasional Paper 30. p. 23.

commodities and an excess demand for bonds at the initial values of income and interest rates.[113] The increased demand for bonds increases the price of bonds, and as such the Keynesian liquidity preference function causes an excess demand for money at the initial level of income.[114] The subsequent decline in the rate of investment will be halted prior to the level necessary for full employment, and thus any excess demand for money and excess supply of commodities with inflexible wages and prices will result in a decrease in output and income. In algebraic terms:

$$W_t = \emptyset\,(\,N_t\,,N_t-1\,) = W^e/_t\,,\emptyset\,(\,N^*,N^*\,) = 0\,, \quad \text{or}$$

$$W_t - W_t - 1 = \emptyset\,(\,N_t\,,N_t-1\,) + W^e/_t - W_t - 1$$

Thus N^* is the steady equilibrium rate of employment, since $\emptyset$ does not contain the rate of inflation, actual or expected, equilibrium is maintained no matter what the rate of inflation, which may be called the natural level of employment.

Therefore in conclusion, Keynes used the concept of expectations to illustrate the distinction between savings and investment. As the price system was not able to equate savings and investment,[115] as savings are essentially a decision to forgo consumption for an undetermined period, the level of investment required to ensure full employment is a matter of chance, unless participants possessed perfect market knowledge of the future.

Thus the lack of equilibrium in Keynes' analysis in the General Theory is an attempt to establish economic growth at full employment at a disequilibrium level of operation, due to the existence of uncertainty and expectations. The acceptance of this fact, reduces the direct role of money in the analysis in favour of the physical interrelationships within the monetary economy, increasing through time. This accommodates the fact that strictly rational behaviour is impossible,

113 Ibid, p. 23.
114 Ibid, p. 23.
115 J. A. Kregel: *An Introduction to Post Keynesian Economics*, Macmillan, Hong Kong, 1973. p. 10.

given uncertainty, and must be compensated for by the conduct of the economy on the basis of accepted convention.[116]

This value of estimation addresses an economic environment with less than perfect information about future events, and emphasises the critical analytical relevance of uncertainty and individual expectations in support of Keynes' argument against conventional Neoclassical theory.

Clearly the works of Keynes bear the strong imprint of the Marshallian tradition from which they sprang. Nevertheless, it has shifted the emphasis of monetary theory to the point where the role of money is defined as an asset with special properties in an uncertain world and has forced recognition of the fact that a monetary economy is fundamentally different from a barter economy. Additionally it provided a simple but comprehensible model of the economy, which not only facilitated the analysis of aggregative problems, but greatly stimulated the development of econometric work with such models. It explained why the competitive capitalist economy does not automatically maintain a satisfactory level of employment and outlined the theory of remedial policy, thereby promoting a revolution in ideas on the responsibilities of government in such a system.[117]

However, Keynes' theory was obviously weak at a crucial point, specifically in its neglect of the influence of capital on behaviour; and its influence has been to distract attention from the role of money in the functioning of the economy. This is not to suggest that Keynesian theory was dislodged by the challenge of Monetarism that was to follow, in anything resembling the way that the Classical theory had been dislodged by the revolution begun by Keynes. It is granted that the Monetarist attack led to some substantial qualifications and amendments to Keynesian theory but no more than that. It has been true for several decades, and remains so today, that an introduction to macroeconomic theory is essentially an introduction to Keynesian theory.

116 The General Theory of Employment: Op Cit.
117 P. A. Samuelson: *Economics*, Second Australian Edition, McGraw-Hill Book Company, 1955. Sydney.

8

The Neoclassical Orthodoxy

The Neoclassical Orthodoxy, or as it is often referred to the Neo-classical Synthesis, is generally accepted as the orthodox inter-pretation of the modern capitalist system. It is considered to be a mainstream analysis which has frequently been afforded the title of 'accepted paradigm', albeit more out of academic convenience than practical relevance.

Two examples of exponents of this paradigm are Paul Samuelson and Campbell McConnell, both having published widely read and accepted introductory texts on the subject of macroeconomic theory. In fact, Samuelson's book *Economics* was first published in 1948, and a new edition has appeared every three years since that date. Additionally McConnell who first published in 1960 is well into his seventh edition.

However the fundamental nature of the analysis presented in the texts remains unchanged. In fact these two writers have cap-tured between them a considerable sector of the market, especially in America, and it is considered probable that the majority of practising economists in America today learnt their introductory economics from one of these authors. By extension it is also worth noting that a significant percentage of those not privileged to benefit from this exposure were subject to texts similar in content to those described above.

Essentially this school of generally accepted reasoning establishes a capitalist system characterised by relatively free and competitive product and resource markets, which determine the overall pattern of production and distribution of goods and services. Deficiencies within the market system are recognised and intervention in its operation by governments in the interest of society in general, is advocated on two principal conditions.

The first point of reason concludes that individual markets may not operate effectively to produce goods and services and then allocate resources in the most efficient manner, from the point of view of society as a whole, or to achieve an equitable distribution of income, and hence goods and services, however that may be defined. Secondly, and as a continuation of this line of reasoning, the aggregate level of economic activity and of employment prices at any point in time, and at the rate of economic growth over time might also be inappropriate, and improvable by government action.[118]

Nearly all conventional economic texts contain sections which analyse the operation of product and factor markets, and incorporate the operation of the economy in comprehensive terms. This process of elucidation also includes the forces determining aggregate levels of economic activity, employment, prices etc. In each case perceived deficiencies of the system are analysed and the role of government in modifying and improving its operation or its issues of economic policy, are discussed at the same time.

Thus McConnell has sections headed, 'National Income, Employment and Fiscal Policy', 'Money, Monetary Policy and Economic Stability' and 'Economic Growth, Analysis and Policy' – all fundamental issues of macroeconomics. Additionally, Samuelson has major sections on the 'Determination of National Income' which incorporates a discussion of economic policy with particular reference to product markets, with an emphasis concerned with public policy.[119]

The relevant passages cover essentially the analysis established in the late nineteenth century by the Neoclassical economists, especially Jevons and Marshall, and the refinements of Chamberlain and Robinson and later economists particularly with respect to oligopoly. Typically there are chapters on pure competition, monopoly, monopolistic competition and oligopoly, as contingent market structures. The deficiencies

---

118 M. Olson Jr.: 'What is Economics?' in J. H. Weaver, *Modern Political Economy, Radical and Orthodox Views on Crucial Issues,* Allyn and Bacon, 1973.
119 P. A. Samuelson: Op Cit.

of the non-purely competitive market structures with respect to economic efficiency in the strict economic sense are recognised.

However, the advantage to consumers of such market structures, which actually typify modern capitalism, are illustrated, particularly the extent to which they are conducive to product improvement and innovation. Moreover, and very importantly, it is argued by way of implication, that firms with structures such as oligopolies are essentially competitive, they still compete, as do firms in pure competition, to create profits by best serving the demands of consumers.[120]

For example in McConnell, the chapter on 'Oligopoly' is concluded by a short extract from *The National Times* entitled 'Consumer Wins In Rental Car War'. It is recognised that governments may need to intervene to improve the workings of such markets from the point of view of the socioeconomic group as a whole. Implicitly it is argued that markets modified along these lines will perform the function of allocating resources to provide consumers with the goods and services they demand.

The macroeconomic sections present essentially the analysis of Keynes. Again it is agreed that intervention by governments, especially in the form of fiscal and monetary policies are necessary, even though the point is usually implicit rather than explicit and in view of the apparent lack of success of such policies. This is particularly evident when it is concluded that this process is often ineffective against the more significant problems of macroeconomics such as unemployment and inflation, and only subjective expectations satisfy the equalities, and provides an opportunity for probability slumps where high variances in the aggregate price levels reduces the responsiveness of output to demand shocks where it can be said:

$$b\,(\,FN - N\,) = Fw - we = 0$$

Overall the conclusions presented by such texts, although again the point is rarely spelt out explicitly, and the absolute position of most orthodox economists, is that the modern capitalist system, as

120 B. Ward: *What's Wrong With Economics?* Macmillan, 1972.

interpreted through mainstream economics, achieves a broadly satisfactory balance between material welfare and individual freedom.[121]

An example may be illustrated where expectations concerning the
general level of adaptive nominal wages are protracted, the adjustment
of the money wage level would be reflected through a lowering of
the natural rate of employment, for the duration of the period where
algebraic wage inflation was smaller than the expected wage rate
inflation. In semi-log-linear terms, where w is the log of the wage
level and w^e is the expected wage level we have:

$$w - w^e = b(N - N) < 0, b > 0$$

$$w^e = hw(_{-1}) + (1-h) w^e (-1)$$

However, since the early 1970s Orthodox economists and mainstream economics itself, have come under increasing attack. In large
part this is a result of the overwhelming evidence that concludes,
without successful refutation, that Orthodox economics has been
manifestly unsuccessful in providing solutions to the principal economic problems such as unemployment, inflation, lower economic
growth and recessionary spirals that have plagued most capitalist
economies in the last decade.

It must be noted that most Orthodox economists are fully aware
of these criticisms, to the extent that introductory mainstream texts
are now recognising that economics is a discipline if not in crisis,
then at least under attack, and unable to provide the answers to a
large number of problems.

Samuelson pits the paradigm of Orthodox economics against the
critiques of Marx, and the conservative libertarianism of writers such
as Hayek and Friedman, and of J K Galbraith. In fact all he does is
briefly review these critiques rather than attempt to defend the framework of analysis he has put forward against them. Although perhaps
this is not unreasonable, given the nature of his work.[122] McConnell
also acknowledges explicitly that his text is basically concerned with

121 T. Balogh: *The Irrelevance of Contemporary Economics*, Weidenfeld and Nicolson, 1982.
122 P. A. Samuelson: Op Cit. p. 918.

the principles of Orthodox economics and has provided a small concession to the Radical critique.

Nevertheless the exponents of this increasingly questionable paradigm still feel presumably, that Orthodox economics presents the most illuminating analysis of the modern capitalist system, where the course of government involvement is clear, and representative of a satisfactory form of political economic organisation.

9

The Neo-liberals

The Neo-liberal chapter of macroeconomic development is an economic paradigm dominated by a group of economists, among whom Friedrich von Hayek and Milton Friedman are the most respected academically. The Neo-liberals confirm that the Neo-classical framework, as it existed prior to the advent of Keynesian macroeconomics, is the most intrinsically valid interpretation of the capitalist system.

However, they are simultaneously opposed to the way that Neo-classical economics developed, within a context of inherent compromises. Specifically the acceptance within the system that free markets produced certain undesirable results, at a product and factor market level, which could be avoided or reduced by the appropriate political economic action, contending that in reality there was no trade off between inflation and growth, as inflation was at all times a monetary phenomenon.

The Neo-liberals also contend that the very fabric of the capitalist system itself has evolved in a distorted fashion, augmented by the subsequent false expectations concerning its proper role, wherein the increasing role of government activity within the legitimate parameters of economic activity constitutes an undesirable influence.

Therefore to the Neo-liberals, it would seem appropriate to accept the principle of Neoclassical market theory as a valid interpretation of the free market system, while recognising, and opposing the development of interventionist government interaction within the system. This latter issue serves to represent the catalyst for the distortion of the founding capitalist tenants and is responsible for the subsequent conflict with an understanding of an economic system based on the free and unfettered operation of markets, where the causal effects between the movement of money supply and subsequent movements in prices is regarded as a central theme.

As a consequence of this admission, Neo-liberals are frequently regarded as being contiguous to the mainstream, with divergent priorities concerning government macroeconomic activity in areas such as the improvement of resource allocation, the establishment of a more efficient distribution of income or the achievement of economic stability. These features are clearly accepted under modern Neoclassical economic theory.

Further, the Neo-liberals are especially opposed to Keynesian macroeconomic policies, and tend to favour Monetarist interpretations. It is, however worth noting that the doctrines of Monetarism are not as clearly articulated as are those of the Neoclassical paradigm or the Keynesian school. The principles of Monetarism are based on the premise that 'money matters'. That is to say, the operation of the economy cannot be understood, except by specific reference to the inherent behaviour of monetary aggregates and the specific stock of money.

Monetarism as a theory has provided a restatement of the 'Quantity Theory of Money' and a renewed emphasis on the role of the quantity of money. This has been described as a counter-revolution by its leading exponent, Milton Friedman. In his article 'The Counter-Revolution in Monetary Theory', he considers that:

> A counter-revolution must be preceded by two stages: an initial position from which there was a revolution, and the revolution.

The initial position is clearly the Quantity Theory of Money, and the revolution in this instance may be interpreted as the contributions of Keynes. In discussing the counter-revolution he claims:

> A counter-revolution, whether in politics or in science, never restores the initial situation. It always produces a situation that has some similarity to the initial one but is also strongly influenced by the intervening revolution. That is certainly true

of Monetarism which has benefited much from Keynes's work.[123]

Therefore, an effective summation of the Quantity Theory position, which is subsequently espoused by the Neo-liberals and other supporters of this paradigm may be condensed to the following propositions. Initially, the demand for money is considered to be a stable function of variables such as the rate of the return of wealth and the rate of change of price and income considerations.

Subsequently there may be a discrepancy between the level of real money demanded and the stock of nominal money supplied at any given price position which will induce a change in the level of expenditure. That is to say, an excess in the supply of money will increase expenditure, as this is the only means available to the political economic authorities for the removal of the excess supply of nominal money, and conversely an excess demand for real money will reduce expenditure.

Finally, a substitution effect may be established whereby portfolio allocation adjustments, from one asset to another are viewed as being weak, and in this instance it is expected that income effects will predominate. Therefore changes in the nominal stock of money will have a translated effect on nominal income levels and pricing levels are likely to be the most significantly affected.

However, the Neo-liberal position does not advocate a political economic policy of continuous activity, which changes in response to all political data as this may be construed as destabilising, as it has the effect of increasing the variances of undesirable phenomena. Friedman cites the classic relationship between the variances O^2_x and the coefficient of correlation between x and p, denoted rxp to illustrate this point.

$$O^2_y = O^2_x + O^2_p + 2rxp\, Ox\, Op$$

Where $O^2_y < O^2_x$ it is required that $rxp < -(\tfrac{1}{2})\, Op\, Ox$. Therefore a more passive policy, defined by $Op = 0$, may be better than

123 M. Friedman: *The Counter-Revolution in Monetary Theory*, Institute of Economics Affairs, Occasional Paper 33, 1970. p. 8.

an activist policy. This becomes especially relevant in view of the proliferation of highly inaccurate pre revision data and extensive lead times effecting relevance.

Therefore, when examining the premise that systematic political economic policy has no substantive effects on real output, and random policies may increase the variability of output, it is considered that the monetary authorities should adopt a constant rate of money growth. Attempts at fine tuning should therefore be rejected, as illustrated through an adaptive expectation hypothesis where any past history of the economy can be constructed given $_{t-1}P^e_t$

$$_{t-1}P^e_t = \lambda P_{t-1} + \lambda(1-\lambda)P_{t-2} + \lambda(1-\lambda)^2 P_{t-3} + \ldots \quad 0 < \lambda < 1$$

In this model it is clear that government policy may have real effects, provided the price level Pt constitutes an exogenous variable over time t–1. However it is also possible to manipulate the level of output relative to its natural rate, through an aggregate supply equation where demand management is reestablished. In this case $P_t - P_{t-1}$ is the actual rate of inflation and $(_{t-1}P^e_t - P_{t-1})$ is the expected rate of inflation, giving

$$U_t = U_n - \beta\left\{(P_t - P_{t-1}) - (_{t-1}P^e_t - P_{t-1})\right\} + \varepsilon_{2t}$$

Clearly the Neo-liberal interpretations are very similar in provenance to those of the nineteenth century liberals, who reached their prescriptive or ideological conclusions concerning the promotion of the welfare of society in all its dimensions. Their theories contended that a liberated economic system, where the government's role was prescribed as being restricted to that level of political economic involvement, commensurate with providing a basic framework in which the free economic system was effectively able to function most efficiently.

As Neoclassical economics developed and an attenuated and increased role of government involvement was facilitated into its infrastructure, the term 'liberal', particularly in America, came to be applied to those who were more liberal in advocating government involvement in economic life. Galbraith for example, who describes himself as a 'liberal' defines Liberalism in the modern American sense, as adopting the view that:

> improvements in welfare and also an attack on vested positions are its central tasks in accepting, or indeed seeking, whatever state intervention it believes to be required for these ends.[124]

As a consequence, Neo-liberals such as Hayek and Friedman, came to be referred to as 'Conservatives'. They were seen to be resisting the changes to ideas and indeed the system itself, implied by an increasing incidence of political economic manipulation within the economy.

As this examination will illustrate, the laissez-faire approach and Monetarism tended to have a substantial degree of synergy. In the 1970s and 1980s it was common for Monetarists to emphasise the importance of market forces and deregulation, with the possible exception of the financial markets, which altered the ground rules for the continuity in the control of the supply of money.

This is best illustrated through the 'real balance effect' where it is assumed that consumption expenditure is not a simple function of real income, but also depends on real money balances where Ct is the logarithm of consumption expenditure. For a given real income, higher real money balances induce higher real consumptions.

$$C_t = c_1 y_t + c_2 \ (\ m_t - p_t \ ) \ c_1 > 0 \ \ c_2 > 0$$

Additionally, it is argued that higher inflation and nominal interest rates reduce $(m - p)^*$, the steady state of real money balances, and feeds back into the goods market condition. Consumption is reduced, and must change if the goods market is to clear in the new steady state of dichotomy, broken between real and monetary sectors. In this context, monetary policy may be said to maximise its effect on the political economic sector as it is employed to affect the steady state levels of all real variables, especially the level of output, employment and the real rate of interest. In the event that the economy is

124   J. K. Galbraith: *American Capitalism*, Penguin, 1963. p. 11.

not in a steady state, provided there remains a real balance effect on consumption, systemic monetary policy will be translated into the goods market, thereby affecting the level of investment required for market clearing.

There has been some postulation amongst Neo-liberals that the real balance effect is a disequilibrium phenomenon, which vanishes in the steady state, as once non-linear models are adopted anything which alters the capital stock, will by definition alter the marginal product of capital. The obvious implications for political economic theory are the relationships to the real rate of interest, as cash pays a zero nominal rate of interest, any policies which alter the expected inflation rate must alter the real rate of return on money. Therefore accepted portfolio or asset equilibrium implies that real rates of return on substitutes such as real capital must also be altered.

Therefore the Neo-liberals are perhaps most commonly referred to as Conservatives, as is anyone who argues for less rather than more government involvement in economic activity. Therefore it is considered that the use of the title Neo-liberal, while not widely employed, is the more accurate of the two.

Milton Friedman for example, discusses this issue in the introduction to one of his major works:

> It is extremely convenient to have a label for the political and economic viewpoint elaborated in this book. The rightful and proper label is liberalism. Unfortunately, as a supreme, if unintended compliment, the enemies of the system of private enterprise have thought it wise to appropriate its I label, so that liberalism has, in the United States, come to have a very different meaning than it did in the nineteenth century or does today over much of the continent of Europe.
>
> As it developed in the late eighteenth and early nineteenth centuries, the intellectual movement that went under the name of liberalism emphasised freedom as the ultimate entity in the society. It supported laissez-faire at home as a means of reducing the role of the state in economic affairs and thereby enlarging the role of the individual; it supported free trade abroad as a means of

linking the nations of the world together peacefully and demo-
cratically. In political matters, it supported the development of
representative government and of parliamentary institutions,
reduction in the arbitrary power of the state, and protection of the
civil freedoms of individuals.

Beginning in the late nineteenth century, and especially after
1930 in the United States, the term liberalism came to be associated with a very different emphasis, particularly in economic
policy. It came to be associated with a readiness to rely primarily
on the state rather than on private voluntary arrangements to
achieve objectives regarded as desirable. The catchwords became
welfare and equality rather than freedom. The nineteenth century
liberal regarded an extension of freedom as the most effective way
to promote welfare and equality; the twentieth century liberal
regards welfare and equality as either prerequisites of or alternatives to freedom.

In the name of welfare and equality, the twentieth century
liberal has come to favour a revival of the very policies fought.
In the very act of turning the clock back to seventeenth century
mercantilism, he is fond of castigating true liberals as reaction-
ary.'[125]

However it is increasingly recognised that Monetarists, and the liberal
community generally, continue to lobby for a reduction in government
regulations and restrictions to permit market forces greater scope to
establish more efficient economic performance and to generate more
wealth. This has obvious implications for the public sector, as tax
revenues decrease and restrictions to work practices such as excessive
trade union practices are countered to facilitate technological enhance-
ment within the economy. The systemic monetary policy will affect the
path along which the economy converges to the steady state under
'perfect foresight' or 'rational expectations', however the concept of a
'strong neutrality theorem' holds only in the exceptional instance
where the real balance effect is completely ignored.

---

125 M. Friedman: *Capitalism and Freedom*, University of Chicago Press, 1962. pp. 5–6.

Additionally, an extension of this theory may be interpreted through supply side economics, which arrives at exceedingly divergent political economic conclusions, from a similar premise that prosperity, as determined by current real income or aggregate employment, depends on the appropriate fiscal and monetary rationalisations.

Clearly supply side economics does not constitute a highly original premise, given that the concept of choice and incentives has been of central consideration since the advent of the Neoclassical paradigm; however it does proffer an interesting political interpretation, given its preoccupation with the macroeconomic policy mix. The consideration of suboptimal policy utilisation, and the implications for controllability, infers the desirability of the implementation of monetary policy as a stabilising factor against higher levels of fiscal intervention. This obviously demonstrates a much reduced short-term perspective of monetary lead times than the Neo-liberals would accept, but additionally affords interesting evidence of a disinflation utility.

However, despite the hybrid inclusion of significant amounts of Neoclassical labour theory, there remains a quantitative imbalance in nominal or real labour market analysis, and inconsistent causal relationships in fiscal implementation, due to empirical inadequacies in complete policy prescriptions. The requirement for a compromise between Neoclassical optimum growth and optimum public expenditure policies in the context of a Keynesian style money wage or price conflict, resulting in less than full employment, cannot be allowed to reside in the domain of rigid exchange rate manipulations, or convenient temporal causative monetary supply policies.

10

The Heterodox View

Any paradigm, even at the height of its reign, has its critics, Hobson and Veblen were two critics of Neoclassical economics at a time when it was widely accepted as a credible explanation of capitalist economic activity. However, as individuals they were very different and they wrote in rather different circumstances. Hobson was English, and most of his original writings spanned the 1890s to the 1930s. Veblen by contrast was American of Norwegian descent and wrote at much the same time, over a slightly narrower period.

Both in their different ways presented a novel interpretation of the socioeconomy and a trenchant criticism of the Neoclassical paradigm. Both rejected the narrow focus of the prevailing economic theory and considered that the socioeconomic structure had to be analysed as a complete entity, contending that the emerging disciplinary barriers between economics, politics, psychology, etc. should be broken down; this view resulted in economists dismissing them as indeed they dismiss contemporary writers who subscribe to similar views, as mere 'sociologists' or even worse, 'journalists'.

Neither Hobson nor Veblen was successful within the academic establishment; Hobson in fact never obtained a post at a University and Veblen made it only to the rank of assistant professor. Further, their views made relatively little impact when they were put forward and were never regarded as a serious challenge to the Neoclassical orthodoxy and the ideology established upon it. It is considered that the reason for this may be attributed in part, in the point made by Canterbery in his discussion of Veblen, which in short, proposes that a ruling paradigm must be reducible to a few basic principles so that it can be passed on in texts and classrooms.

It has been said that the essence of an orthodoxy of any kind
is to reduce the subtle and sophisticated thoughts of great men
to a set of simple principles and straightforward slogans, so
that more mediocre brains can think they understand them well
enough to live by.

Neither Hobson nor Veblen produced such a reducible orthodoxy.
While it might be exaggerating somewhat to refer, as Canterbery
does, to 'the simple mechanics of Newtonian Neoclassicism', it is
true that compared to the Neoclassical theory of the market system,
the ideas of Hobson and Veblen seemed vague, diffused and in-
conclusive.

However the echoes of both their ideas are to be found in the
writings of contemporary critics of Orthodox economics, who are
now receiving somewhat more attention than was accorded Hobson
and Veblen. They argue that economic activity could only be understood in terms of its wide historical, cultural and social context. They
thus reject Canterbury's 'Newtonian mechanics' as shedding no useful
light on how things really work.

Clearly they are not only dissenters from Orthodox economic ideals, but additionally they pursue a different direction to the Neo-liberals concerning aspects of the inherent political economic nature of
the system itself. Conversely, they do not challenge the legitimacy
of the system in such a fundamental way as the Radical political
economists in terms of the accepted, if not literal, meaning of the
word 'Radical'. Therefore they still represent a significant development in macroeconomic theory in their own right, and are typical of
the diverse group of economists known as 'institutionalists' or perhaps
more generally as Heterodox economists and establish the inevitable
extension of their basic concepts through more widely accepted Heterodox writers such as J K Galbraith.

Veblen was the ideological father of the 'evolutionist-institution-
alist' school of thought, a concept which is uniquely American. John
Kenneth Galbraith is probably the best known contemporary economist in this tradition started by Veblen. Galbraith is a 'liberal' in the
twentieth century connotation of the term, who has been critical of

many aspects of the American economic system. As well as questioning the standard theoretical interpretation of it, he has tended to accept, with a degree of fatalism, much of its basic nature; however his reformists doctrines may be linked directly to the concepts espoused initially by Veblen, albeit with much more credibility and widespread acceptance than Veblen ever enjoyed.

Veblen considered that the socioeconomic function had to be analysed as a coherent entity. He was concerned with the cumulative growth of changing social conventions in the broadest sense. This implies not only material conventions, but additionally customs, social habits, modes of thinking, belief and style of living. Like those who have followed in his tradition he was concerned with questions such as the provenance of the economic organisation of society, the direction of its evolution and future possibilities.

He criticised Orthodox and Neoclassical theory as being too concerned with static values and price phenomena, while misconstruing the usefulness of a theory which simply tried to identify timeless economic 'laws' divorced from the evolutionary process of the development of economic organisation. Veblen was also critical of the hedonistic psychological base upon which the whole of Neoclassical economic theory was derived. That is to imply that the notion of 'economic man' maintained that motivation was achieved not solely by pecuniary interests, but by other instincts as well.

The ideas that Veblen developed himself, as alternative explanations and analyses of a capitalist society to the Neoclassical economics ideal, revolved very much around one central idea. This central notion was the sharp contrast between 'business enterprise' and the 'machine process'. By the machine process he meant the technical methods used in producing goods, the relations of these methods to each other in the factory and, most importantly, the habit of thought which working with machines and directing their operations formed. The machine process served to satisfy man's basic material needs and also served as an outlet for the instinct of workmanship. Its object was 'serviceability', for Veblen there was something inherently rational about it.

However, the machine process functioned in the context of business enterprise. While the scope and method of modern industry are given by the machine, it is the businessman:

> who has become a controlling force in industry, because, through the mechanism of investment and markets, he controls the plants and processes, and these set the pace and determine the direction of movement for the rest. As near as it may be said of all human power in modern life, the large businessman controls the exigencies of life under which the community lives.[126]

This was a critical point of evolution because in Veblen's view the businessman's principal aim was indeed to maximise profits, serviceability was only secondary.

The consequence of this reasoning leads to the conclusion that the interests of industry and community welfare were sacrificed in favour of business interests. In effect he argued that the vast accumulation of knowledge and technology, which ought to be the common heritage of all men, was being abused and subsequently exploited to further the economic interests of a small capital controlling class. There was thus a conflict between business and industry, and between the principles of vendibility and serviceability or, to use Galbraith's formulation of sixty years later, the 'private' and the 'public' interest.

One of the results of the later stage developments of the system was, in Veblen's view, a situation of chronic depression. The reason for this was that in advanced countries, such as America and Britain

> the advancing efficiency and articulation of the processes of the machine industry reached such a good pitch that the cost of production of productive goods has ... persistently outweighed such readjustment of capitalisation as has from time to time been made.

---

126   T. Veblen. The Theory of Business Enterprise', Romano and Leiman, *Views on Capitalism*. pp. 276–277.

The situation was in essence one of overproduction and attending declining rates of profit in which depression was inevitable. The solution lay either in increased unproductive consumption through waste public spending on armaments, public edifices etc, or in the elimination of cut throat competition which kept profits down, through monopolistic tendencies. Veblen was sceptical that increased extra-industrial spending would fill the gap and concluded that:

the tendency to consolidation is irresistible.

Hobson reacted to this issue through the question of the response of economic policy, especially as the total output of the modern industrial system was so great, and the balance formed the third major category which Hobson called unproductive surplus. It was the unproductive surplus which he generally referred to simply as the surplus.[127]

The way that national income, and most particularly the unproductive surplus was inefficiently distributed was explained by Hobson in terms of 'economic forces'. This was derived from various hindrances to perfectly equitable bargaining power among the owners of various factors of production, and subsequently conferred upon these proprietorial negotiators an element of scarcity which allowed them to receive a return exceeding that necessary to evoke the productive power of the factor and to that extent earn surplus income.

Such a view may not seem very remarkable today, but it was put by Hobson in a book entitled *The Economics of Distribution* in 1900 when it was hardly fashionable to criticise the incomes of the more elitist professions. Hobson saw the surplus, or more specifically, what was done with it, as the essence of all socioeconomic problems. In his words:

The abuse or uneconomical use of the surplus product is the source of every sort of trouble or malady of the industrial system,

127 See: 'John A. Hobson: Economic Heretic', *American Journal of Economics and Sociology*, July 1978.

and the whole problem of industrial reform may be concluded in terms of a truly economical disposal of this surplus.

He was one of the first writers to develop a macroeconomic theory of unemployment. At the end of the nineteenth century and in the early twentieth century it was considered that unemployment could only occur as a result of the gradual adjustment of market forces. Hobson, however, argued that given that the contemporary industrial system had a chronic tendency to produce a surplus, the proprietors of the factors of production, of which there was a natural or contrived scarcity, found themselves with incomes in excess of what was needed or even desired to spend on consumption.

Accordingly they applied it directly or indirectly towards capital accumulation. There resulted, in other words, a chronic tendency towards over saving, under consumption and as a consequence, over-production when these excess savings were applied to capital accumulation. From this, Hobson developed a theory of 'periodic crises', which alluded to a cycle of booms and depressions in the economic system and further suggested that periods where unemployment was a problem were endemic to the capitalist system.

Hobson also applied his theory of surplus to the issue of imperialism. Indeed he is probably best known for his book in 1902 on this subject. He argued, in essence that imperialist activity was simply the political economic manifestation of the economic need for outlets for surplus savings or surplus production, resulting from those savings being directed to capital accumulation.

The solutions to these problems lay, in Hobson's view, in converting surplus income either into wages which could be spent in raising the standard of living of workers, or into public revenues which could be spent in raising the standard of public life. He saw the surplus as the sole legitimate source of public revenue and a source that should be tapped and applied to maximise the public interest, instead of in the socially malignant ways that it was being applied by the private people to whom it accrued.

He thus concluded that all taxes should be devised to impact upon the unproductive surplus. He recognised the difficulty of applying this principle in practice and admitted that the greater part of the surplus was not clearly traceable and measurable. However the principle pointed fairly clearly to the desirability of a major emphasis on direct taxation, particularly a graduated personal income tax, supplemented by inheritance taxation, and to the general undesirability of indirect taxation except on goods and services which were indications of superfluity of income. Once again the conclusions do not seem especially remarkable today but were quite revolutionary in many respects at the time Hobson put them forward.

Hobson also spelt out what he saw as the rationale of the labour movement in terms of the surplus. He argued that trade unionism should be understood as an organised attempt to divert the unproductive surplus, or unearned income, into wages. This is seen as a result of the circumstance where, normally labour was the weakest claimant to the surplus and it was necessary for labour to enhance its bargaining power. This end was served in Hobson's view, not only by contribution, but by trade union support of social reforms over a whole range of issues from land legislation to education and in particular to what he called 'anti-destitutionalism measures'.

These are just some of Hobson's more interesting theories. However he also kept up a running critique of Neoclassical economics.[128] This critique centred on the method of what Hobson called 'marginalism', a term he coined which subsequently gained widespread acceptance. He saw economic theory as:

reducing economic life ... to a number of infinitesimal activities and transfers of matter (and) a number of infinitesimal acts of choice, both registered in the monetary medium.

Money being a single absolute standard of values and infinitely divisible fluid, the concrete economic objects that it handles, measures and moves have a similar character of the affairs of the community at large falls by common consent into the hands of

---

128 Hobson's critique of neoclassical economics was spelt out most fully in a book published in 1926 entitled *Free Thought in the Social Sciences*, especially in chapters II and III of part II ('NeoClassical economics in Britain' and 'Marginalism in Neo-Classical economics').

businessmen and is guided by business considerations; modern politics is business politics. Representative government means, chiefly, representation of business interests.'[129]

Moreover it was generally accepted by people that there was a solidarity of interest between them and business. The consequence of this was 'government for business ends'. One example of this, indeed 'the extreme expression of business politics', was in Veblen's view, the then current policy of war and armaments.

In his final book *The Engineers and the Price System* written during the 1920s, Veblen virtually predicted that engineers and skilled workmen, the guardians of the machine process, provoked beyond endurance by the inefficiency of business proceedings, 'vendibility' being given precedence over 'serviceability' would take into their own hands the operation of the industrial system, and operate it solely in the interests of mechanical efficiency and serviceability. The revolution of the engineers never came of course, and if one accepts the Galbraithian arguments they have now been immersed into the business enterprise and become part of the 'technostructure'.

This is one the central themes behind the Galbraithian paradigm, and has been widely expanded on in several of Galbraith's major works such as *American Capitalism* (1952), *The Affluent Society* (1958), *The New Industrial State* (1967), and *Economics and the Public Purpose* (1973).[130] In *Economics and the Public Purpose* the arguments of the previous books, particularly *The Affluent Society* and *The New Industrial State* are expanded upon, consolidated and enhanced.

In particular he developed the important concepts of producer rather than consumer sovereignty, of the corporation as the main

---

129 Ibid.

130 *Economics and the Public Purpose* is the most complete of his books and may not unreasonably be compared to the great 'Principles' books of the nineteenth-century economists, to Marx's *Das Kapital* and (in the heterodox tradition) to Veblen's *Theory of Business Enterprise* (1904) or Hobson's *Work and Welfare; A Human Valuation* (1911). It is the sort of wide-ranging book that has become a rarity, ones of such scope being found only in the form of introductory text-books which are a rather different animal. *Economics and the Public Purpose* draws on and integrates Galbraith's previous work and is the best summary of his main ideas.

planning force in the system, of the technostructure as the main force in the corporation, and of the subordination of the state to the corporation. After a summary of the main characteristics of Neoclassical economics, Galbraith then proceeded to present his theory of the modern industrial capitalist system.

Much of the argument is very similar to that of the 1967 analysis, however the evaluation is subsequently refined to effectively distinguish between what he terms as 'the market system' and 'the planning system' as two distinct parts of a modern capitalist structure. The latter was his central concern in *The New Industrial State*; it constituted a relatively small number of very large corporations which undertook the bulk of economic activity;

> making up the remainder of the economy are around twelve million smaller firms, including about three million farmers, whose total sales are less than those of the four largest industrial corporations; just under three million garages, service stations, repair firms, laundries, laundromats, restaurants and other service establishments; two million small retail establishments; around nine hundred thousand construction firms; several hundred thousand small manufacturers; and an unspecified number serving the multivariate interests of an advanced society in what is collectively called vice.[131]

The conceptual difference between the two systems is determined by whether the enterprise is;

> fully under the command of an individual and owes its success to this circumstance,

or whether;

> the firm ... without entirely excluding the influence of individuals, could not exist without organisation.[132]

---

131   J. K. Galbraith: *Economics and the Public Purpose*, Pelican, 1975. p. 43.
132   Ibid, p. 44.

In Galbraith's view the planning system is the dominant one. Socioeconomic goals, and hence the development of society, is determined by the planning system. This influence is reinforced because, as Galbraith said, 'the planning system exists in the closest association with the state'. He frequently described this relationship as symbiotic.

Additionally, the foundations of this argument were laid in *The New Industrial State*. The conclusion, stated badly, is that the government responds actively to the desires and needs of the planning system. The process works most effectively through the public bureaucracy;

> Public regulatory bodies, it has long been observed, tend to become the captives of the firms that ostensibly they regulate. This is because the rewards of cooperation between the technostructure and the regulatory agencies normally outweigh those of conflict. The compliant regulatory body accedes to the needs of the technostructure, the latter supports or, in any case, does not oppose, the continued existence and needed budget expansion of the regulatory body. The aggressive regulatory authority, by contrast, invites public scrutiny of its needs. And, since its conflict is with the technostructure – it will be widely regarded as being in conflict with sound public policy. When it questions actions of the technostructure – the safety or quality of its products, the truth of its advertising – it is interfering with the natural prerogatives of private enterprise or hampering the growth of those innovations which, being the goals other technostructure, are the foundations of sound public policy. Acquiescence, even if it risks criticism for being useless, may be better bureaucratic policy.[133]

However one of the greatest sources of authority in the planning system is the capacity to influence public policy.

> The technostructure consists of corporation executives, lawyers, scientists, engineers, economists, controllers, advertising

---

133   Ibid, p. 160.

and marketing men. It has allies and satellites in law firms, advertising agencies, business consulting firms, accounting firms, the business and engineering schools and elsewhere in the universities. Collectively these are the most prestigious members of the national community. They are generally the most affluent in a society that measures worth by affluence. Their view on public policy is the view that commands the solemn respect, and with full allowance for the eccentric and often well rewarded heresies hitherto mentioned, it is the view which reflects the needs of the planning system. It cannot be supposed to involve conflict with the public interest. What serves the technostructure – the protection of its autonomy of decision, the promotion of economic growth, the stabilisation of aggregate demand, the acceptance of its claim to superior income, the provision of qualified manpower, the government services and investment that it requires, the other requisites of its success – is the public interest. Papal infallibility was powerfully served by the fact that the Holy Father defined error. The assurance that public policy will infallibly serve the technostructure and the planning system is similarly assisted by the ability of the technostructure to define the public interest. In recent years the existence of an accepted and strongly self-serving source of public policy has become generally recognised. It is called the establishment.[134]

These arguments illustrate one of the principal conclusions of *Economics and the Public Purpose* and indeed throw some light on the choice of the title. The perceived influence of the planning system on public policy implies that the 'planning purpose', which is indicative of the goals of the technostructure, is readily transformed into the ambition of government policy. The planning purpose therefore, becomes the public purpose, the latter being equated in a general sense with the 'public good' or the 'public interest'. As a result the government, far from being an independent force operating in a

134 Ibid, pp. 162–163.

neutral way to secure an increase in the public welfare, comes to
reflect, and this applies both to the legislature and more particularly
to the bureaucracy, the goals and needs of the corporate sector of
the economic system.

The final section of the book is called 'A General Theory of
Reform'. The aim of the reforms suggested by Galbraith are, in the
most general sense, to make the operation of the economic system
accord with the public purpose. The initial proposition is what Galbraith calls 'the emancipation of belief'.

> Until this has happened, there is no chance for mobilising the
> public on behalf of its own purposes in opposition to those of
> the technostructure and the planning system. The latter will
> continue to pursue its purposes under the protection of the
> belief that its goals are those that best serve the public.

The second pre-requisite to reform is the emancipation of the state;

> It is only with a public state as opposed to one possessed by
> the planning system that ... reforms ... can be carried through
> with the retrieval of the state for the public purpose.

The way is thus clear for the implementation of a number of
policies involving greater control by the state. The increased control
is inevitable and necessary if the system is to be made to work for
the public good. Therefore, by necessity the reforms are spelt out in
considerable detail. Galbraith divides them into three categories; his
own summary follows:

> There is first the need to enhance radically the power and compe-
> tence of the market system – to enhance affirmatively, its devel-
> opment in relation to that of the planning system and thus to
> reduce from this side the systematic inequality in development as
> between the two systems. This includes steps to reduce the in-
> equality of return as between the planning and market systems –
> to improve the bargaining power of the market system and reduce
> its exploitation by the planning system. This is here called The

New Socialism. Necessity has already brought the new socialism farther into being than most suspect.

Then comes policy in relation to the planning system. This consists in disciplining its purposes – in making these serve not define, the public interest. This means restricting resource use in the areas of over-development redirecting the resources of the state, to serve not the planning system but the public, asserting the higher purposes of the environment, making technology serve public and not technocratic interest.

Finally the economy must be managed. The problem is not to manage one economy but two, one that is subject to the market and one that is planned by its constituent firms.[135]

The complete details of Galbraith's reforms are spelt out in chapters 22 to 30 of *Economics and the Public Purpose*. However, it is possible to note one general point; frequently in these chapters Galbraith suggests that his reforms are determined by circumstances, which he seems to interpret as the inevitable progression of events, which we will be compelled to adopt. Indeed he argues that most of his principles are in fact already being implemented incipiently.

The majority of his contentions, however from agricultural price fixing aimed at enhancing that segment of the market system, to wage and price controls as part of the overall management of the two systems, run contrary to the accepted economic doctrine and are acknowledged with reluctance. In Galbraith's view the emancipation of belief would allow us to see that they are both necessary and desirable.

As noted above Galbraith has come in for criticism from both the mainstream and the Radicals. From the former has come some rather vitriolic criticism for his 'unscholarly', and 'unscientific' style. He has been called a 'non-economist's economist' and is readily dubbed a mere 'populariser' or 'journalist'.

Two introductory passages from reviews of *The New industrial State* indicate the general tenor of mainstream attitudes:

135 Ibid, pp. 221–222.

One must begin with a candid recognition that the academic reader
of Galbraith's books is under a strong temptation to react nega-
tively to the author's style and method of discourse. He waives
the scholarly conventions in favour of a rhetoric which is designed
to appeal to the lay reader. But the stylistic techniques he employs
to this end increase the difficulty of grasping the substance and
structure of his thought and work against a fair and objective
appraisal of it by an orthodox scholarly mind. Galbraith is satiric,
scornful and flippant. There is often a sneer at his pen point. He
makes use of much verbal fret work and delights in the sudden
reversal. He loves paradoxes and aphoristic generalisations so
much that he often allows a witty sentence to stand when it really
requires retooling in order to carry accurately the content of his
thinking. An even greater barrier, especially to the economist, is
that Galbraith is simplistic.

There are innumerable passages in his books which make one
ache with vexation at his over generalisation, exaggeration, and
stereotype. His treatment of the 'conventional wisdom' of older
economists, one of his favourite pegs on which to pin a donkey's
tail, reflects an occluded memory of some old lectures in the
history of economic thought that would have been better if completely forgotten. His treatment of what modern economists think
is derived largely from the Arcadian world of the elementary
textbook. When he himself deigns to be analytical along the lines
of conventional economic theory, he is often sloppy. In addition
to this, he carries on a continuous vendetta against the economists
of the economic establishment.[136]

The second review continues the tone;

More than once in the course of his new book Professor
Galbraith takes the trouble to explain to the reader why its
message will not be enthusiastically received by other economists.

---

136   S. Gordon: The Close of the Galbraithian System', *Journal of Political Economy*, July-August,
1968.

Sloth, stupidity, and vested interest in ancient ideas all play a part, perhaps also a wish – natural even in tourist class passengers – not to rock the boat. Professor Galbraith is too modest to mention yet another reason, a sort of jealousy, but I think it is a real factor. Galbraith is, after all, something special. His books are not only widely read, but actually enjoyed. He is a public figure of some significance; he shares with William McChesney Martin, the power to shake stock prices by simply uttering nonsense. He is known and attended to all over the world. He mingles with the Beautiful People; for all I know he may actually be a Beautiful Person himself. It is no wonder that the pedestrian economist feels for him an uneasy mixture of envy and disdain.[137]

On the other hand the Radicals believe that Galbraith's model is merely a:

kind of new, streamlined apologetic for monopolistic capitalism.[138]

Both the mainstream and Radical critics have come up with detailed objections to aspects of Galbraith's analysis; however, these go somewhat beyond the scope of this investigation. Nevertheless he did initiate a style of analysis, critical of Neoclassical economics, which was eventually to produce what many people regard as a far more serviceable explanation of the real world.

137 R. M. Solow: 'The New Industrial State or Son of Affluence', in *The Public Interest*, Number 9, 1967.
138 P. M. Sweezy: 'Utopian Reformism', in *Monthly Review*, November, 1973. p. 3.

11

Radical Political Economy

R adical political economy is a term used to describe a corpus of analytical concepts concerning economic organisation, with specific reference to modern capitalism and its orthodox interpretation. This paradigm developed essentially as a reaction to the Orthodox system itself, which Radical political economists interpret as being a fundamentally unsatisfactory form of political economic organisation.

The analysis is generally in the Marxist tradition of a social analysis built on the over determined interaction between the fundamental and subsumed classes.[139] However it is only since the late 1960s that the number of academics who regard themselves as Radical political economists, has reached respectable numbers. Additionally, the body of writings which is 'radically' critical of Orthodox economics and modern capitalism itself, and through which has evolved a radically different analysis and view of modern capitalism and its salient characteristics, has grown rapidly. As it is perhaps to be expected, it is rather difficult to find a concise summary of what constitutes a Radical political economy. The writings of Franklin, in *American Capitalism; Two Visions* is one of the few books that attempts such a summary view.

Franklin attempts to discover the incentive behind the revival of the Radical political economy since the mid-1960s. He explains this in terms of

---

139   W. J. Waters and E. L. Wheelwright: 'Universitty Economics – a Radical Crittique', from E. L. Wheelwright and Frank J. B. Stilwell (eds.), *Readinqs in Political Economy*, Volume 1, ANZ Book Company, 1976. p. 21.

events and issues that have forged a 'climate of opinion' conducive to critical thought.[140]

In short there is evidence of discontent or concern with a number of aspects of the capitalist system. Some of these are specifically American, but then that is where the main developments in Radical political economy have taken place, in addition to the growing disquiet within the mainstream itself.

The latter factor he argues has eased the path for the Radical interpretation;

> that some basic aspects of mainstream theory are being doubted by leading members of the economic establishment affords radical political economists an opportunity to reach a larger audience than at any time since World War II.[141]

In short, the fact that the Radical political economy has developed over the last three decades to the point where there is now a reasonably coherent body of thought, that can be referred to as the 'Radical paradigm', can be explained in terms of the level of dissatisfaction with both the system itself and the Orthodox system of thought which it interprets. Therefore it is entirely reasonable to interpret Radical political economy as a discipline which differs from mainstream economics in several critical ways. A brief summary of these characteristics are outlined below.

Fundamentally, Radicals are interested in historical dynamics. Institutional change is accepted as inevitable and the nature of this change must be studied. Moreover, and very significantly Radicals advocate change. Specifically with regard to capitalism they see themselves:

> on a historical journey to end, rather than to stabilise capitalism; they are working for the establishment of a socialist society. Their theorising is regarded as integral to their advocacy of fundamental change.[142]

---

140 Franklin: *American Capitalism: Two Visions*, Chapter 7. p. 105.
141 Ibid, p. 111.
142 Ibid, p. 114.

In other words there is a deliberate incorporation of ideology as an integral ingredient within the theoretical base; they advocate a society founded on,

participatory planning, public ownership, elimination of production for profit, and a genuinely egalitarian redistribution of wealth.

They do not purport to be undertaking a value-free study of economic activity which, as they see it, implicitly involves an acceptance of the status quo.

Radicals are therefore committed to an interdisciplinary approach, as they do not believe that economics can be studied in a vacuum, and that it must be interpreted within the context of the social and political structure of the socioeconomic evolution and its historical development. Radicals reject the market and favour 'planning' as the principal coordinating mechanism facilitating decisions concerning economic activity are made. It has been proposed that even within the Neoclassical paradigm, planning rather than the market, at present determines much of the economic activity. However it is in fact private planning, which is typically representative of the business corporation. The Radicals argue instead for public planning which is conducive to a decentralised democratic, participatory structure. Radicals consider that specific structural economic arrangements such as the pattern of ownership and the control of resources have significant implications for the distribution of economic power; power to influence both economic and political considerations. Consequently it is considered that power must be explicitly incorporated in the analysis.

Inevitably, for Radicals the issue of the distribution of wealth and income takes on a much greater significance than for their mainstream colleagues. This, it seems, is relevant to the previous consequence because wealth and income and the distributions thereof are seen to have important implications for the possession and exercise of political power. On a more general level, Radicals believe in a society where:

there is mass participation in decision-making and the equal
sharing of income and wealth.[143]

They envisage a society based on what Franklin terms 'solidarity'
rather than 'individualism' and 'competition', and they argue that
capitalism is incompatible with this belief.

At the most general level Radicals believe, and incorporate in their
analysis, a view of human nature which holds that humans are socioeconomic animals, and that their motivations and their welfare
must be interpreted in terms which are primarily social and which
encompass non-economic as well as purely economic criteria. This
contrasts with the view implicit in mainstream economics that;

> individuals are naturally acquisitive and motivated primarily
> by their narrowly defined economic interests.[144]

This discussion outlines the ideological foundations of Radical
political economy and in that sense therefore defines its intention. It
is clear that Radical political economy has its intellectual origins in
'the spirit and logic' of the Marxist schema. For this reason the
majority of Radical political economists are quick to point out that
they also regard themselves as Marxists.[145] However, that is not to
imply that they subscribe totally and uncritically to everything Marx
said. However it would seem that they do subscribe to what Franklin
claims is the:

> intellectual power, scope, capacity to bring together a broad
> range of apparently unrelated phenomena, economic and non-
> economic, into a unified framework ... the integrated, 'inter-
> disciplinary approach'.

Clearly the interdisciplinary approach is important; coupled with
a commitment to the transformation of the socioeconomic order

---

143 Ibid, p. 120.
144 Ibid, p. 122.
145 R. C. Edwards, A. MacEwanetal: 'A Radical Approach to Economics: Basis for a New
Curriculum', in *American Economic Review*, Volume 60, number 2, May 1970. p. 361.

prevalent within the mainstream paradigm. In a book titled *The Capitalist System: a Radical Analysis of American Society*, which is regarded as one of the most important contributions to the Radical literature, the authors have commented:

> We do not find everything that Marx or his followers have written to be useful, or even relevant or correct. Nonetheless our primary intellectual debt is to Karl Marx.[146]

Therefore it is difficult to offer a complete and logically self-contained summary of Radical political economy, however it is possible to present an accurate picture of its provenance.

To this end, Radicals quote from the writings of Ernesto (Che) Guevara to provide a statement which best described their position:

> When asked whether or not we are Marxist, our position is the same as that of a physicist or a biologist when asked if he is a 'Newtonian' or if he is a 'Pasteurian'. There are truths so evident, so much a part of people's knowledge, that it is now useless to discuss them. One ought to be 'Marxist' with the same naturalness with which one is 'Newtonian' in physics or 'Pasteurian' in biology, considering that if facts determine new concepts, these new concepts will never divest themselves of that portion of truth possessed by the older concepts they have outdated. Such is the case, for example, of Einsteinian relativity or Planck's quantum theory with respect to the discoveries of Newton; they take nothing at all away from the greatness of the learned Englishman. Thanks to Newton, physics was able to advance until it had achieved new concepts in space. The learned Englishman provided the necessary stepping stone. For them ...
>
> The merit of Marx is that he suddenly produces a qualitative change in the history of social thought. He interprets history, understands its dynamics, predicts the future, but in addition to predicting it which would satisfy his scientific obligation, he

---

146 The book is written and edited by Richard Edwards, Michael Reich and Thomas Weisskopf (Prentice-Hall, 1972).

expresses a revolutionary concept; the world must not only be interpreted, it must be transformed.[147]

The matter tends to reduce to semantics particularly where the word 'Radical' is concerned; literally the word means 'going to the root of', which presumably any person wanting to analyse and interpret the economic organisation, or political influences of society wishes to do.

However, it would appear it is quite possible to be a political economist and in a certain sense a Radical political economist without subscribing to the views of Marx; except in the most general sense, by merely holding that an integrated, interdisciplinary approach to analysing economic organisation is necessary, and by adopting a reformist, rather than revolutionary position, such as the case of Joan Robinson, a contemporary of Keynes.

Hobson, Veblen and the institutionalists following Veblen, including Galbraith could also be regarded in this context. However, having said that political economists who subscribe to the Radical paradigm generally acknowledge a substantial debt to Marx and call themselves Marxists, Galbraith does neither of these. Indeed the Radical analysis of capitalism is often referred to as the 'Neo-Marxian' analysis.[148]

The Neo-Marxian analysis of contemporary American capitalism is best summarised by Paul Baron and Paul Sweezy in their book titled *Monopoly Capital* (1966). This is regarded as the most comprehensive and influential effort to adapt the Marxian schema to the contemporary situation.[149] The principal adaptation is seen as an effort to cast the analysis in terms of the multi-national corporation, to recognise that the modern capitalist economy is dominated by a relatively small number of large business units. Marx's original analysis was couched in the more familiar terms of a competitive rather

147 Ibid, p. X.
148 M. Olson, Jr: 'What is Economics?' from J. H. Weaver, *Modern Political Economy: radical and Orthodox Views on Crucial Issues*, Allyn and Bacon, 1973. p. 22.
149 P. Baron and P. M. Sweezy: *Monopoly Capital*, Pelican, 1968.

than a monopolistic model, even though Marx was one of the first writers to predict the tendency towards concentration.

The concept around which the Baron and Sweezy's analysis revolves is that of the 'surplus'. The surplus is related to, but not identical to, the original Marxian concept of 'surplus-value'. The relation between surplus and surplus-value is in fact not particularly clear and the Baron and Sweezy concept seems much closer to that of Hobson.[150] Expressed in the most general terms, the essence of the Baron and Sweezy notion of surplus is that it is a measure of the economic system's ability to produce more than it needs in the sense of some socially necessary minimum. Baron and Sweezy then argue that the modern capitalist system tends to produce an ever-larger surplus.

The central problem the system faces is thus to utilise or absorb the surplus, to find outlets for all this productive potential. The penalty of not finding outlets is considered to be stagnation and unemployment. The three main possibilities for utilising the surplus are: increased consumption achievable through greater sales efforts and built-in obsolescence; public welfare expenditure on utilities such as health, education, transport facilities; and foreign investment and defence expenditure which are often, though not necessarily, related.

Baron and Sweezy are not hopeful that these means of absorbing the surplus produced by the American economy will be successful. Indeed they consider that some will only exacerbate the problem. Therefore they deduce that the prognosis for the system is grim. Baron and Sweezy do not, however, forecast the inevitability of revolutionary action as being necessary to overthrow the system from within as did Marx; for a while at least those individuals adversely affected can be kept powerless or bought off. The major threat it is considered, will come from the third world.

---

150 The Hobsonian concept of the surplus was discussed in Chapter 10; the relationship between Marxian 'surplus value' and the Baran and Sweezy 'surplus' has been examined in detail in William J. Barclay Jr. and Mitchel Stengel, 'Surplus and Surplus Value', *Review of Radical Political Economy*, Number 1, 1977.

Therefore, in as much as the Baron and Sweezy thesis contains the main outline of the Radical analysis of capitalism, specifically American capitalism, it is necessary to take the next step to consider specific issues within Radical political economy.

One issue of particular concern to Radical political economists is the labour process which in general terms may be interpreted as the circumstances under which people work and the way that rewards for work are determined. In their view, mainstream economic theory treats labour as a commodity to be bought and sold on the market. The rewards for selling labour are determined according to the productivity of that labour and individuals have considerable control over this productivity, for example by improving their skills and education. Radicals, however argue that the weakness of this approach is that work arrangements are to a large extent outside of the control of the individual and are largely determined by the social structure. They have therefore developed an alternative framework of analysis of the labour process which provides a different way of explaining how, ultimately, income is distributed in a capitalist society.[151]

Another issue that attracts the interest of Radical political economists is that of economic growth. The definition of economic growth is quite simply the rate at which the total output of goods and services in an economy, as measured by GNP, grows from one year to the next. Radical political economists believe that the mainstream preoccupation with economic growth is a result of its interpretation as a means to solving some of the problems of the existing economic system. Growth is also seen as a necessary part of capitalism if the system is to continue in its present form.

In fact the growth mania of the 1950s and early 1960s, resulted in profound criticism in the late 1960s and early 1970s by substantial supporters of mainstream economics.[152] In 1967, E J Mishan of the London School of Economics published *The Cost of Economic Growth*; shortly afterwards the Club of Rome published its study

151 Franklin: Op Cit. pp. 178–91.
152 Ibid, pp. 199–200.

The Limits of Growth which concluded that if the present rate of growth continued the pressure on non-renewable resources would lead to a series of catastrophes in a relatively short time. Radical economists recognised some of these anti-growth arguments but their analysis of the growth issue was undertaken on a somewhat different plane.

Initially Radicals argued that:

growth and its prerequisite profits are to business as heroin is to the addict.[153]

A businessman in the capitalist system is inevitably hooked. They argue that business in fact concedes this, hence in part the Orthodox acceptance of the 'need' for growth. The capitalist need to accumulate is like the addict's need for a 'fix'.[154]

Secondly, their belief that one can not automatically assume that all components of GNP are necessarily good, and thus that more is necessarily better. To Radical economists, much of the growth mania is a 'waste' mania, and the present composition of GNP reflects the giant corporation's increasingly unproductive role.

Inflation is another issue which is treated in a very different way within the Radical paradigm.[155] A major feature of the Radical explanation of the present mix of inflation and unemployment is that it is part of the general theory of capitalist development, whereby the Radicals argue that the mainstream analysis has been forced to rely on exogenous variables, such as factors not inherent in the functioning of the capitalist system as such, to explain what has gone wrong.

Inflation and unemployment are seen, in the Radical analysis, as an inevitable outcome of capitalism's modus operandi. One important feature of the system which, it is argued, must be taken into account as an endogenous variable is deficit spending by governments;

153 Ibid, p. 211.
154 Ibid, p. 211.
155 D. Ward: *Toward a Critical Political Economics: a Critique of Liberal and Radical Economic Thought*, Goodyear, 1977.

the government is part of the larger system and part of the system's problems, and it cannot therefore be relied upon as an independent corrective force.[156]

Governments have been forced to establish increasing onerous budget deficits to close the gap between actual and potential output. The consequence of this, though it is not well or fully argued, is a self perpetuating chain of inflationary debt and refinancing in the private sector and an economy increasingly more vulnerable to cyclical dips.

The reason for the necessity of sustained and increased deficits is to be found in the industrial lure of modern capitalism. The monopoly sector is dominant and,

> increasingly calls upon the state to socialise (subsidise) costs by investing in research and development projects, highway construction, industrial parks, office buildings, utilities and education.[157]

The funds for this must come from either taxes or deficit spending and the latter is clearly politically more convenient. On the micro economic side, the very fact of the monopoly of firms on the one side and organised labour on the other, results in an inflationary wage spiral. One consequence of this is an increasing tendency to resort to labour-saving technology and unemployment. The general conclusion is that there are contradictions in the system which inevitably result in both inflation and unemployment. The state must grow to keep the system in motion but in obtaining the finance to grow it produces inflation.

A final theme, but one that plays a key role in Radical political economy, is imperialism.[158] The accepted definition of imperialism as defined by most Radicals is:

156 Franklin: Op Cit. p. 231.
157 Ibid, p. 237.
158 W. J. Waters and E. L. Wheelwright. Op Cit. p. 26.

the sustained effort to maintain third world countries in economic positions subordinate to, dependent upon, and complementary to the United States.[159]

This is considered by some to be a rather narrow interpretation, particularly in so far as it pertains only to the relationship between the United States, which is sometimes a preoccupation, and third world countries; however it is the context in which much recent analysis of the more general phenomenon of economic hegemony has been undertaken.

The difference between the mainstream and Radical analysis of imperialism is that the former does not regard the phenomenon as an inherent part of capitalist development. It is recognised that advanced capitalist countries exert economic and political dominance over other nations, however the basic causes are not recognised as economic or as being inherently related to the capitalist system. However, Radicals argue that the development of the capitalist system,

> driven by the profit motive and concomitant desires to accumulate, tends to extend the nation's economic interests far beyond its (geographical) borders.

And in addition;

> once such interests have been established, or even recognised, the superstructure acts to protect and nurture them.[160]

Imperialism is a difficult concept to rationalise in a macroeconomic investigation, however within the context of political ambition it is clearly important. Additionally it is clear that there is by no means any single clear Radical theory. The Neo-Leninist view is widely accepted by Radical pundits, where the multi-national corporation is a reflection of the need for businesses in an advanced capitalist system to expand the geopolitical territory in which it operates. To realise this goal they require governments to 'protect the free world',

159   Franklin: Op Cit. p. 247.
160   Ibid, p. 254.

and this produces the more overt political consequences generally associated with imperialism.

Therefore it is quite a challenge to offer a complete and logically self-contained summary of Radical political economists, however it is possible to present a summary of their important conclusions. There has been a considerable amount of work done in recent years and it is quite a massive task to synthesise this into a form that can be presented in a text-book comparable to Samuelson's *Economics*; Franklin's *American Capitalism* is one of the few texts that attempts this.

12

The Mainstream

One of the few replies to the Radical attack on Neoclassical economics, and certainly the most comprehensive, is that by Assar Lindbeck in *The Political Economy of the New-Left, an Outsiders View*. Lindbeck is a Swedish economist, on the 'liberal' wing of the mainstream;[161] that is, he is not as McFarlane puts it in his view of Lindbeck 'one of the troglodytes of laissez-faire' but accepts that a certain amount of government intervention in a basically free-enterprise economy is desirable. He is therefore in broad agreement with the political economic philosophy of social democracy capitalism, as practised in his native land. At the same time he accepts the framework of conventional or orthodox Neoclassical economics as the most useful system of thought for analysing economic organisation and activity.

It is from this perspective that he reviews the economics of the 'new Radicals'. It is therefore considered reasonable to regard the political economy of the new-left that Lindbeck discusses as synonymous with the 'new Radical' economics or 'Radical political economy' as has been discussed prior to this point, However there is a slight problem at this juncture. One could infer from some comments from Lindbeck,[162] as in fact Samuelson does infer,[163] that the new-left is a wider and more diffuse movement than Radical economics.

Lindbeck claims he is 'focusing on the economics of the new-left', separating out and scrutinising in isolation a small subset of new-left

---

161 A. Lindbeck: *The Political Economy of the New Left: an Outsiders View*. p. 184. The term 'Liberal' is of course used in the twentieth-century sense.
162 Ibid, p. 2.
163 Samuelson: Op Cit. p. xviii.

ideas.[164] It should be noted however, that Lindbeck's critique is based on work completed in 1968 and 1969 and there has been quite a considerable amount of work achieved within the Radical political economic framework in the two decades since then. Whether this would alter Lindbeck's description and evaluation of the political economy of the new-left is a difficult question to answer. It would be reasonable to assume the answer would be positive from a substantive view, but not from a fundamental perspective.

Lindbeck offers an original description and critique of the new-left's critical analysis, first of Orthodox economics and secondly of the capitalist system itself. As such it may be regarded as a mainstream reply to the Radical attack. This may be interrupted to imply that Lindbeck has attempted to make a contribution to the field of comparative economic systems, by virtue of the critiques he offers of the present economy. Lindbeck believes that once an evaluation of an economic system is undertaken, the analysis inevitably becomes involved with questions of what an economic system should do, and whether alternative economic systems, real or hypothetical, do these things better or worse than the alternatives under examination.

It is within this framework, established by Lindbeck, that the theories of those concerned with issues in the economic theory of capitalism and socialism were able to establish a greater degree of credibility and widespread acceptability. One economist to benefit from this introduction was Michael Kalecki, although some would argue that Lindbeck may in fact have benefited from him. Kalecki who died in his native Poland in 1970, made a number of seminal and highly original contributions to pure and applied economic theory, especially to the theory of economic dynamics and income distribution.

The main body of Kalecki's work may be summed up in the posthumous publication of his selected essays, *Selected Essays on the Dynamics of the Capitalist Economy; Volume 1,* and *Selected Essays on the Economic Growth of the Socialist and Mixed Economies;*

164 A. Lindbeck: Op Cit. p. 6

Volume 2.[165] Both works constitute a return to mainstream analysis. Volume 1 contains Kalecki's contributions to the macrodynamic theory of effective demand; economic growth, fluctuations and distributions of national income and his prediction of the regime of political business cycle. Volume 2 opens with Kalecki's fundamental attempt to construct a basis for theory of growth in a centrally planned, socialist economy. Part II is concerned with the basic problems in the theory of investment efficiency and the scope of the evaluation of such efficiency in a socialist economy. Part III deals with the economic problems of the mixed economy.

Interestingly, and contentiously the essence of Kalecki's work establishes him as having historical precedence in the discovery of the 'General Theory of Employment'. It fundamentally indicates a superiority in analytical originality to that of Keynes. Without any contact with Keynes, Kalecki discovered independently all the basic components of Keynes' analytical system and put it to good use. In addition to making a number of important contributions, such as integrating the theory of aggregate output determination, price and distribution, Kalecki's system is dynamic. Viewed from the standpoint of a rigorously constructed macro-dynamic model and considering the use to which the analytical construct was put, Kalecki's contribution appears to be more seminal than Keynes.[166]

Clearly both Kalecki and Keynes had a genius for the academic translation of realities of life. They shared unusual insights into how things actually worked and provided keen theoretical insights to extract the essence of the problems. It is perhaps this common facility which actually enabled them to come to similar conclusions. However Kalecki lacked the status, authority and influence enjoyed by Keynes. Therefore as is often the case, Keynes' contribution to the change

---

165 M. Kalecki: *Selected Essays on the Dynamics of the Capitalist Economy.* Cambridge, Cambridge University Press, 1971; and *Selected Essays on the Economic Growth of the Socialist and Mixed Economy*, Cambridge, Cambridge University Press, 1972.
166 G. R. Feiwel: 'Issues in the Economic Theory of Capitalism and Socialism: Michael Kalecki's Contribution Over Four Decades', in *The Indian Economic Journal*, Volume XX, Number 2, October–December 1972. p. 153.

in the mode of thinking of the economic profession and on policy making was greater than that of Kalecki.

However, both Kalecki and Keynes provided a solid foundation for the generalisation of the 'General Theory of Employment' and both had a varied impact on the course of development of the theory;[167] it may be noted that in some respects Kalecki's version of the 'General Theory' is narrower and more compact, but it is not a less precise analysis of the modus operandi of the aggregative output theory. There is still much to be learned from this work.

In his classical theory of the business cycle, Kalecki introduced fundamental and importantly, dynamic properties into the analysis. The notable examples include the time lag between investment decisions, orders and actual realisation, and the determinants of investment decision making.[168]

The investment realisation time lag explains the cumulative character of the process of expansion and contraction. An increase in investment decisions constitutes investment activity and via the multiplier effect the expansion of national income. The growth of income makes investment more profitable and influences the undertaking of more investment decisions. Consequently an upswing is accelerated. However, while each investment increases effective demand and encourages new investment, it also establishes a capacity-creating effect and conversely at the same time discourages more investment.

Therefore the rise in investment cannot continue indefinitely. When the level of investment exceeds the level necessary to maintain the stock of capital intact, the cumulative process of expansion is counteracted by the capacity creating effect of new investment. As investment ceases to rise so does the level of current profit. However, the productive capacity, investment being positive, continues to expand and the new investment competes with the capital stock of older vintage. As profit is stationary, sales cease to expand, while capital stock enlarges. Profit yielded per unit of capital falls and so do investment decisions.

167   Ibid, p. 154.
168   M. Kalecki: 'Trend and Business Cycles Reconsidered', in *Economic Journal*, June, 1968 p. 265. Reprinted in *Selected Essays on the Dynamics of the Capitalist Economy*. p. 168.

Thus it becomes clear that the boom cannot endure. An inverse process to that of expansion takes place and by that mechanism expansion is transformed into the cumulative contraction process. When the level of investment falls below that necessary for replacement, the stock of capital shrinks. As a result return per unit of investment, the marginal efficiency of investment increases. Therefore, eventually, the process of capital stock shrinkage will be arrested.

Thus boom gives rise to recession, recession to depression, depression to recovery, and recovery to boom. The expansion of the productive apparatus hampers the upward cumulative movement and brings it to an end and to the inevitable slump as investments exert retarding effects when positive or the acceleration effect is negative.

This leads to the conclusion that in a neutral economy, negative investments extricate the economy from the slump. This is obviously the weak point in his theory, just as the concept that the acceleration of capital stock is responsible for the turning point in the boom may be regarded with scepticism. The premise remains that the growth of national wealth contains the seeds of retardation of the growth rate of economic activity. However, during a considerable part of the cycle the additional wealth actually proves to be merely potential in character, as the accumulated capital is substantially under utilised. It becomes productive only in the successive upsurge.

Thus the theory asserts that disinvestment or decapitalisation of national wealth, spurs prosperity, breeds forces that put an end to the shrinkage of capital, and stimulates an increase in investment. The shrinkage of capital stimulates the upswing and again the expansion of capital contains the seeds of depression.

While his earlier writings were clearly influenced by the severity of the experience in the early 1930s, in the subsequent development of the argument Kalecki generalised the theory and made allowances for the relatively weak impact of the capital destruction effect.

Moreover, he allowed for the special importance of fluctuations in inventories during the course of economic fluctuations. Later Kalecki also incorporated those factors in his analytical construct. He thus introduced a certain 'corrective influence' and focused increasing attention on the trend component that investment fluctuates along the long-run trend line.

Kalecki sought to advance theoretical development in the field towards integration of growth and cyclical processes. The main lines of development were evident in the successive recasting of the argument. He advanced an original, provocative, but somewhat sketchy, theory of long-run development trends, and its determinants both of trend and cycle. Innovation plays a cardinal role in transforming the static system subject to cyclical fluctuation around the zero level of capital accumulation into one subject to growth trend.

Later Kalecki became sceptical about separation of the business cycle into a pure cycle in a trendless economy and attempted to implement a novel approach to the problem;

> I myself approach this problem in my 'Theory of Economic Dynamics' and my 'Observations on the Theory of Growth' in a manner which now I do not consider entirely satisfactory: I started from developing a theory of the 'pure business cycle' in a stationary economy, and at a later stage I modified the respective equations to get the trend into the picture. By this separation of short-period and long-run influences I missed certain repercussions of technical progress which affect the dynamic process as a whole. I shall now try to avoid splitting my argument into these two stages just as much as applying the approach of moving equilibrium to the problem of growth.[169]

While the investment function as proposed in Kalecki's early model is acknowledged to be a close foreshadowing of many modern developments in econometric research, he appears never to have reached a fully satisfactory solution. In his own words;

> It is interesting to notice that the theory of effective demand, already clearly formulated in the first papers, remains unchanged in all the relevant writings, as do my views on the distribution of national income. However, there is a continuing

---

169 Ibid, p. 163.

search for new solutions in the theory of investment decisions, where even the last paper represents, for better or for worse, a novel approach.[170]

It may be said that post-Keynesian capitalism avoided a sharp depression as a result of timely and effective government intervention resulting from adequate interpretations facilitating its involvement in matters largely beyond its control. However it is often established that this occurred in a context far remote from full and efficient utilisation of national economic resources. Clearly the pattern of the postwar political business cycle that Kalecki envisaged as early as 1943 was on the whole prophetic. The concept of the political business cycle, was strikingly in advance of its time. Indeed if not borne out in all its respects, the most remarkable feature of the theory is the degree to which Kalecki did foresee the essence of post-war developments.

170 M. Kalecki: Op Cit. pg viii.

13

Post-Keynesian Economics

The Post-Keynesian economic phenomenon is a fundamentalist paradigm which is currently attempting to establish itself as a credible academic entity in the face of more conventional and accepted intemporal preferences of economic interpretation.[171] It is considered the provenance of this theory originates in the belief that the original views of Keynes are fundamentally incompatible with Orthodox theory. It is a concept legitimised in the belief that over the past 60 years many of Keynes' critical insights into the workings of a modern, technologically advanced economy seem to have been ignored or misconstrued, with the result that there has been little fundamental change in the way economists perceive the systemic theoretical operation of causal mechanisms and utility specifications.

The subsequent belief that the impact of the 'Keynesian revolution' was largely abortive, is characteristically most endemic among those who were closely associated with Keynes at Cambridge during the 1930s. One such colleague was Professor Joan Robinson, who as a student of Keynes, came to know, understand, interpret and to extend the basic tenets of Keynesian economics. Additionally, the associates of Keynes, were ultimately enjoined by increasing numbers of economists from subsequent generations, especially at Cambridge, who initiated an increasing number of attempts to develop a more complete

---

171 The term neo-Keynesian has also been used. It should also be added that Keynes's is only one of the contributions upon which the new approach is based. Certainly the work of Michael Kalecki has been no less important than that of Keynes; and to the extent that the new approach rests on the theory of value which grows out of the work of John von Newman and Piero Sraffa, those names need to be mentioned as well. Indeed, to Marxists the work of Sraffa is seen as being the most fundamental of all, and they al likely, as a result, to refer to the new approach as neo-Ricardian.

'generalisation' of the 'General Theory'[172] This represents a reaction
to the perceived inadequacies of the dominant strand of economic
theory that Robinson has labelled 'Neo-Neoclassical economics',
which Robinson claims is a contemporary illustration of Neoclassical
economics.

This generalisation may be said to represent, in Thomas Kuhn's
words, 'a new paradigm',[173] and since it extends the analysis set
forth in Keynes' *Treatise on Money* and *The General Theory*, it may
be termed Post-Keynesian.

However the reaction from the contemporary Neo-Neoclassical
economists has been a resolute and deafening silence. It would appear
that few economists are aware of the major works that have contributed
to the development of this infant paradigm and fewer still, even among
those likely to be sympathetic, seem to be aware of the possible significance of this potentially new and innovative approach.[174]

Part of the problem may be attributed to the diversion created by
the 'Cambridge controversy' over the theory of capital.[175] While it
is true that some of the elements of Post-Keynesian theory became
better known through the criticisms by Cambridge (England) of the
treatment of capital in the Neo-Neoclassical growth models favoured
by Cambridge (Mass.), the debate has nonetheless left the misleading
impression that the transatlantic adversaries have only a negative
critique to offer. Typically this is characterised as a critique which
is applied only to a highly abstract capital theory and which only
persons skilled in mathematics and econometrics could understand.

172   J. Robinson: *The Rate of Interest and Other Essays*, London, Macmillan, 1952.
173   T. S. Kuhn: *The Structure of Scientific Revolutions*, Chicago, University of Chicago Press,
1962.
174   A typical example is the American tradition which is more representative of Keynesianism
than of Keynes's own work. See for example the distinction set out by Axel Leijonhufvud in *On
Keynesian Economics And The Economics of Keynes*, New York, Oxford University Press, 1968.
Even now he admits that his own interpretation is based on Walrasian rather that Marshallian
principles and, thus, not a valid representation of Keynes's work. The distinction he draws, however,
still holds true.
175   G. Harcourt: *Some Cambridge Controversies in the Theory Of Capital*, Cambridge University
Press, 1972.

Thus the building blocks of Post-Keynesian economics in modern economic analysis may be interpreted in two negative achievements of Post-Keynesian economics as emphasised by Robinson; the critique of Neo-Neoclassical economic theory, and the critique of Neo-Neoclassical growth theory.[176] Initially, Robinson objects to the way in which Neo-Neoclassical economic theory dresses up the old Pre-Keynesian ideas in modern garb and pretends that they are scientific propositions, rather than ideological prejudices.

Further, Robinson takes exception to the Walrasian foundations of Neo-Neoclassical economic theory in that it is based on a timeless static approach. Finally there is a point of contention with the prevailing concept of capital and the analysis of economic transition and economic growth that is implied by the Neo-Neoclassical concept of capital.[177]

Robinson's views about the older Pre-Keynesian notions of the inherent stability and self regulating properties of the economy are trenchantly expressed in this extract from a joint paper with Frank Wilkinson published in the first issue of *The Cambridge Journal of Economics*:

While prosperity ruled, the deeper insights of the Keynesian revolution were lost to view. The bastard Keynesian doctrine, evolved in the United States, invaded the economic faculties of the world, floating on the wings of the almighty dollar. (It established itself even among intellectuals in the so-called developing countries, who have reason enough to know better.) The old orthodoxy, against which the Keynesian was raised, was based on Say's law, there cannot be a deficiency of demand.

Spending creates demand for consumption goods, while saving creates demand for investment goods such as machinery and stocks. Keynes pointed out the obvious fact that investment is

176 J. Robinson: 'The Second Crises of Economic Theory'. *The American Economic Review*, Volume LXII, Number 2, May 1972. p. 7.
177 J. Robinson: 'History Versus Equilibrium', in *The Indian Economic Journal*, Volume XXI, Number 3, January-March 1974. pp. 202–13.

governed by the decisions of business corporations and public
institutions, not by the desire of thrifty householders to save. An
increase in household saving means a reduction in consumption;
it does not increase investment but reduces employment.

According to the bastard Keynesian doctrine, it is possible to
calculate the rate of saving that households collectively desire to
achieve; then governments, by fiscal and monetary policy, can
organise the investment of this amount of saving. Thus Say's law
is artificially restored, and under its shelter all the old doctrines
creep back again, even the doctrine that a given stock of capital
will provide employment for any amount of labour at the appropriate equilibrium real-wage rate.

If so, unemployment occurs only because wages are being held
above the equilibrium level. (In the third world, it is just too bad,
because the equilibrium wage corresponding to full employment
is far below the level of subsistence.) Keynes was diagnosing a
defect inherent in capitalism.

Kalecki, who developed the same theory independently, went
much further and held that without radical change capitalism was
incapable of rectifying the defect. But the bastard Keynesians
turned the argument back into being a defence of laissez-faire,
provided that just the one blemish of excessive saving was going
to be removed.

The view to which Robinson objected was expressed in this statement by Paul Samuelson;

> The findings of our macroeconomic analysis rejects both the
> classical faith that laissez-faire must by itself lead to Utopian
> stability and the pre-World War II pessimism that classical micro
> economic principles have become inapplicable to the modern
> world. Instead we end with the reasoned prospect that appropriate
> monetary and fiscal policies can ensure an economic environment
> which will validate the verities of micro economics, that society
> has to choose among its alternative high-employment production
> possibilities, that paradoxes of thrift and fallacies of composition

will not be permitted to create cleavages between private and social virtues or private and public vices.

By means of appropriately reinforcing monetary and fiscal policies, a mixed economy can avoid the excesses of boom and slump and can look forward to healthy progressive growth. This being understood, the paradoxes that robbed the older classical principles dealing with small-scale 'microeconomics' of much of their relevance and validity will now lose their sting. The broad cleavage between microeconomics and macroeconomics has been closed by active public use of fiscal and monetary policy.[178]

Neo-Neoclassical economic theory establishes its nascent micro economic foundations in the Walrasian general equilibrium theory which is in the European tradition of economic analysis based on the writings of Leon Walras. Walrasian general economic theory differs from the Marshallian analysis which employed the partial equilibrium technique of analysis in which it is assumed that, what we would now refer to as the exogenous macroeconomic variables, are given and the analysis of a part of the economic system, say the demand for a particular commodity, then proceeds by considering a change in one endogenous economic factor.[179] The Marshallian partial equilibrium technique is in its own way a very powerful form of analysis and in the hands of a master exponent like Marshall is capable of generating profound economic propositions; however it attempts to deal with dynamic forces and problems within a static framework of intemporal substitution.

The Walrasian approach is fundamentally an 'Exchange economy' in which a given endowment of commodity is distributed randomly or arbitrarily among consumers who then exchange or trade with each other to achieve their preferred utility specification. This Exchange economy model is employed quite effectively by J R Hicks' in his *Value and Capital* and Don Patinkin's *Money Interest and Prices*. However, the Walrasian Exchange economy is postulated

178 P. Samuelson. Op Cit. p. 348.
179 J. Robinson: Op Cit. p. 3.

within the context of an absence of a production equation; given that modern general equilibrium theorists find it difficult to weld production activities on to the Exchange model, and therefore it inevitably commits the sins against which Robinson has cast so many stones. The sins are those of ignoring real historical time intemporal preferences and of dealing with all problems in a static framework.[180]

Radford in *Economica* (1947) points out that Robinson has criticised the Exchange model by claiming that the only form of economic organisation it adequately represents is a Second World War prisoner-of-war camp. The essential criticisms of this representation of an economic system are threefold.

The initial criticism concerns the concept of real time; that is, time in a historical context is ignored or more strictly speaking has no logical place in this scheme, whereas the existence of real historical time is an endogenous fact which has to be taken into account in modern economic conventional time additive analysis. Many economic problems occur in real life because of the existence of time. In real life the present is the link between a determined past and an uncertain future. This is one of the reasons, of course, that Post-Keynesians place so much importance on uncertainty and expectations in their dynamic analysis.

The second criticism of the Exchange model is that the equilibrium prices determined in one trading period have no rational relevance to economic activity in succeeding time periods. Therefore equilibrium values become entirely irrelevant in the case of a secondary distribution of production outputs. The existing set of prices do not, and cannot provide any information concerning the exchange possibilities and exchange values in subsequent periods. Obviously the determining set of prices is irrelevant to any future distribution.

The third criticism is that to characterise an economy which uses one commodity for a medium of exchange as a 'monetary economy' entirely misses the point as to what exactly constitutes a monetary

---

180   J A Kregel: 'Economic Methodology in the Face of Uncertainty: The Modelling Methods of Keynes and the Post-Keynesians', in *The Economic Journal*, June 1976, volume 86, Number 342. p. 220.

economy. An Exchange economy in this context is therefore essentially a barter economy.[181]

An important feature of Post-Keynesian economics is the analysis
of inflation which emphasises the conflicts in society over the distribution of income. The Post-Keynesian analysis is in stark contrast to
that of the Monetarists who regard inflation as a monetary phenomenon,
which can be resolved by resorting to the appropriate monetary adjustments by the political economic authorities. Post Keynesian analysis
by contrast, regards inflation as a real phenomenon. The essence of
this view is captured in the following extract from the article by
Robinson and Wilkinson which has been referred to previously:

> A major point in the analysis of Keynes and Kalecki, which
> the complacent economist seems to have overlooked, is that
> there is no meaning to be attached to the concept of equilibrium
> in the general price level. The Keynesian revolution began by
> refuting the then orthodox theory that there is a natural tendency
> in a market economy to establish equilibrium with full em-
> ployment. If men were in fact out of work, in the orthodox
> view, it must be because wages were above the equilibrium
> level and profits were too low. Unemployment on this view was
> 'voluntary' because trade unions could easily get rid of it by
> accepting lower wage rates. Keynes agreed that a rise in profits
> would increase employment, but he agreed that a general cut in
> money-wage rates would reduce the price level more or less in
> proportion, so that neither profits nor employment would increase.
> If this argument is correct, it must follow that to raise money
> wages will increase prices, even if there is unemployment.

Consequently Post-Keynesian economic analysis considers that income policies have to play an important role in the construction of
macroeconomic policy. Most Orthodox economists of the Neo-
Neoclassical school regard income policies as a palliative and a last
and rather desperate attempt to deal with inflation. The insight into

181   J. Robinson: Op Cit. pp. 202–213.

the problem was established by Kalecki who saw the difficulties inherent in maintaining a continuous state of full employment. Kalecki's predictions maintained that if full employment was maintained for some years, then there would be a subsequent shift of economic and political power towards wage earners. Unless the economic and political institutions of society changed to accommodate the new realities, there would be a conflict within society over the distribution of income.[182] Wage earning groups would seek to obtain a higher share of total income and this action would-be invariably resisted by the owners of capital. Obviously the Post-Keynesian view is that money wages and money wage rates are the important variables in analysing inflation. In this view, the labour market determines money wages and the real wage rates are determined by the economic system in which the aggregate price level is in turn determined by the interplay of a number of economic forces, including the pricing policies of oligopolistic industries.

Clearly a central aspect of wage behaviour which Post-Keynesians consider to be very important is that a conflict over relative shares within the wage earning group can be inflationary.[183] This must be seen in the context that income policies have generally received negative publicity; they have been regarded as Canute like attempts to stem the tide of wage demands. Additionally, it cannot be denied that nearly all attempts to implement an incomes policy in developed Western economies have been less than successful.

Nevertheless the Post-Keynesian analysis regards an incomes policy as a necessary ingredient in a recipe for a return to an economic performance of high activity and low inflation.[184] The requirements

182 R Lekachman: *Harper's*, Volume 254. Number 1521, February 1977. pp. 35–40.

183 Kregel: *The Reconstruction of Political Economy: An Introduction to Post-Keynesian Economics*, New York, Wiley, Halsted Press, 1973, Chapter 11.

184 It is necessary to stress that Pasinetti strictly confines his analysis to the long period; and that the main thrust of his argument, notwithstanding the response from critic (e.g. Meade; Meade and Hahn; Samuelson and Modigliani) was to show that the distribution of income between wages and profits as well as the rate of profits is determined by the natural rate of growth divided by the capitalists' propensity to save, independently of any 'productivity' of capital (no matter how it is defined) and indeed independently of anything else.

for such an incomes policy are that it applies to all incomes, that it is considered by all parties to be fair and that it is permanent. Too often, incomes policies have broken down because they were seen as confidence tricks designed to place the full burden of adjustment on specific groups in the economy or were taken as the easy option, a make-believe policy, which the authorities accepted because they lacked the resolution to implement harder more constructive options. A critical analysis of British incomes policy given by Tarring and Wilkinson in the *Cambridge Journal of Economics* (1977), points to the failure of government policy to effectively use the breathing space gained in the short time by a successful incomes policy.

In the Post-Keynesian analysis, an income policy has to form part of a sociopolitical contract, a compact in which, in return for imposing constraint on the growth of money incomes, the government clearly contracts to undertake supportive policies to keep the level of aggregate demand at the full employment level. At a basic level, the social compact should involve the following elements; agreement from organised labour not to press for wage claims in excess of a pre-determined figure; an agreement on the part of the government to maintain real living standards so that excessive wage claims are unnecessary; an agreement on the part of the government to sustain a high level of aggregate demand and economic activity; and an agreement by the government to control non-wage and salary forms of income.[185]

An incomes policy of this type has to come to terms with the key problem in the community which enables inflation to continue unless economic activity is unduly depressed. That problem is the one of obtaining a consensus over the distribution of income and wealth in the community. A consensus in this context would be seen as part of a strategy towards genuine socioeconomic change, a development

185 J Robinson: *The Accumulation of Capital*, London, Macmillan, 1956. pp. 404–406 or Kador 'Alternative Theories of Distribution', in *Revolutionary Economic Studies*, 1956, reprinted in Kador *Essays on Value and Distribution*, London, Duckworth, 1960. It is relevant to mention that in regard to one of the issues that had been raised, Kaidor explicitly introduced corporate share finance and the concept of the 'valuation ratio' in incomes policy estimation.

which reconstructs old institutions to cope with the requirements of permanent full employment.

Without such an income policy the dilemma for economic policy is that as economic activity expands from a recessionary level, the pressure on wages held back by the suppression of economic activity become too much to resist and the wage/price spiral is initiated again. The medium term outlook for keeping the rate of inflation low in these circumstances must be regarded as poor unless positive attempts are made to implement an incomes policy which can command widespread support and which is not based on class divisive lines. The legal and institutional barriers to such an incomes policy are far less restrictive than the social and political forces which have to be overcome before an implementation may be effected.

It is necessary to inquire at this point exactly how such an income policy would be orchestrated. The Post-Keynesian analysis has been rather short on specific proposals, however there has been widespread discussions of proposals for the implementation of income policies without substantial institutional changes and by utilising present economic mechanisms.[186] One example is the Tax Incentive Incomes Policy, proposed by Weintraub and Wallich, which would impose a progressive surtax on company incomes, if a company granted wage increases greater, on the average, than a national norm established by the government.

However, perhaps the most imaginative of all these proposals is that by Lerner in *Challenge* (1977), which is based on an earlier insight of Seidman. This proposal envisages a target of price level stability, that is, zero inflation. The mechanism proposed by Lerner is that the government would issue wage increase permits providing for an increase in the wages bill equivalent to a predetermined figure. Such permits would be distributed to employers in proportion to their wage bills; each employer would be required to hold the number of permits equal to the wage increase that he pays. The permit would be exchangeable or hired on a free market. Employers who wanted

186 J. A. Kregel: Op Cit. pp. 209–225.

to increase wages by more than the predetermined figure would be required to hold the corresponding additional permits which could be obtained only by buying them or renting them from employers who raise wages by less than the determined figure and are left with surplus permits.

Therefore in conclusion it is obvious that Post-Keynesian economics is an evolving infant paradigm in economic theory. It is not an easy comparison to make with the Neo-Neoclassical model as there is no single Neoclassical model with which Post-Keynesian theory may be compared. The Arrow-Debreu elaboration of the basic Walrasian model is different from the Marshallian partial equilibrium model emphasised in intermediate price theory courses, and the latter is distinguished from the Swan-Solow aggregate growth model.[187]

However, in effect the majority of these Neo-Neoclassical models share certain common features. Indeed, it is the very existence of these common features that facilitate a comparison with Post-Keynesian theory, yet not all the different versions display all of the common features, just as not all Post-Keynesian models have every one of the characteristics outlined above.

Thus, in a heuristic sense it may be assumed that the term Post-Keynesian economic theory represents a theory of pronounced cyclical patterns superimposed on a matrix of clearly discernible secular growth rates. This position is defined as institutional factors determine a historical division of income between residual and non-residual shareholders, with changes in that distribution depending on changes in the growth rate; where only the past is known, and the future remains uncertain; discretionary income must be equal to discretionary expenditures; imperfect markets with significant monopolistic elements exist; and it seeks to explain the real world as observed in empirical terms.

The last point reflects the distinction made by Korai between theory, in the strict definition as understood by the natural sciences,

---

187 V Chick: 'The Nature of the Keynesian Revolution: A Reassessment', in *Australian Economic Papers*, Volume 17, June 1978, Number 30. p. 17.

implying some general statement about the empirically observable world, and theory as the basis for an optimal decision rule.[188] The distinction is an important one, as the understanding of those who use the initial model often seem to be talking in the past, or failing to communicate with those who employ the alternative model. The problem of communication is, of course, compounded when the Neo-Neoclassical theory is used for a purpose for which it is not suited, that of explaining the real world.

Once the quite different purposes which Post-Keynesian and Neo-Neoclassical theory are meant to serve are clearly understood, certain other differences between the two theories begin to fall into place. For example, the willingness to make assumptions, so evidently at variance with the available evidence is less clearly an anomaly when the objective is to define an optimal decision rule rather than to explain the world as it is. At the same time, however, the quite different purposes that Post-Keynesian and Neo-Neoclassical theory are meant to serve makes even more problematical the already difficult task of determining which of these two models is superior for analysing a modern, market-orientated economy. As Kuhn's work established, it is difficult to choose between alternative paradigms, especially when the more recently established option is still in an inchoate state, even if there is agreement that the purpose of a theory is to explain the empirically observable world. When there are two alternative paradigms, each designed to serve a quite different purpose, the task of choosing between them is further complicated.

188 J Kornai: *Anti-equilibrium: On Economic Systems theory and the Tasks of Research*, New York, American Elsevier, Amsterdam and London, North Holland, 1971.

14

Conclusion

In conclusion it is evident that the causal historical imperatives most significantly responsible for influencing macroeconomic doctrine in a teleological sense, have had intimate and profound implications for the attendant political economic theory. The genesis of these developments may be essentially attributable to differing philosophical prejudices and inevitably differing interpretations of socioeconomic reality; however it is considered that this situation has created one fundamental issue of concern that threatens to compromise the very integrity of the discipline, that is readily apparent to any student of political economics. This may be illustrated in the subsequent proliferation of clearly substantiated, conflicting agendas inherent within the plethora of alternative paradigms, which inevitably is bound to manifest itself as a self-inflicted credibility crisis, threatening to undermine the actual viability of macroeconomic theory as a practical consideration in political theory. Indeed one may be forgiven for assuming the discipline itself may be descending into a state that students of chaos theory would refer to as atrophy.

The competing macroeconomic models may frequently be differentiated as a result of their diverse expectation assumptions, which tend to be internally inconsistent. There is clearly a fundamental requirement for expectation formulation, as a process of decision rule, since empirical data on present and future expectations are not quantifiable, and must therefore be interpreted through econometric modelling substitutes. As we have seen, in the absence of an acceptable model of endogenous expectation revision, political economic policy evaluation has a propensity to be highly misleading.

Therefore while it is widely conceded that a contemporary crisis exists, there is still considerable disagreement concerning the true extent and exact nature of the crisis. In part, this reflects the differing interpretations concerning positive economics, or the perception of how the economy actually works, but it is also reflects differing normative positions or subjective value judgments. The established, entrenched exponents of the Neoclassical school which, as has been illustrated, has been the dominant school for almost half a century, assert that there is no crisis per se, and claims further that there exists only a typical confusion, which is characteristic of the majority of scientific disciplines as they attempt to establish their foundations within the natural processes.

However, a substantial body of critical contention asserts that the predominant body of Keynesian macroeconomics, in fact the very concept of macroeconomics itself in the precise definition of the term, should be called into question. This is essentially considered to be an extension of the revisionist process that requires a return to the fundamental definition of political economics, typified by the Marginalist school in the writings of Ricardo, Adam Smith or even Karl Marx. This assertion has also been expanded on by those who would regress further, to the point where it is possible to re-establish economic theory as a subordinate branch of political philosophy, and therefore create a 'new economics'.

It is considered that this approach has limited merit, apart from the initial attraction of solving contemporary dichotomies, by simply abolishing those characteristics that do not fit conveniently into the parameters allocated. Given that it seeks to eliminate a vast body of 'work' that has culminated in the political economic foundations that constitute our current economic legacy. It is considered that these reformationist impulses are in effect, elaborate attempts to regress to some original and purer source of economic interpretation, that has been obscured by the intellectual complexities and rigours of the modern economic and political environment.

However inclinations of this type are not considered appropriate within the context of the preservation of the credibility of the discipline as it would be construed as an aberration within alternative sciences. Instead it would be more appropriate to regard established theories as the foundations to provide a theoretical base from which the discipline may successfully evolve, and therefore maintain a position of relevance against contemporary political economic requirements. This form of development is especially necessary where the aggregate knowledge is, in some sense cumulative, which is essentially necessary in order to establish the concept as an academic discipline, as opposed to some form of rational enquiry which is devoid of established intellectual credibility.

The political economy is tasked with supervising a system that is long overdue for a fundamental restructuring, characterised by instability and the potential for systemic failure given three basic causal influences: the existing regulatory framework; the emergence of highly volatile interest rates and inflation rates, and the application of information processing technology to the financial sector. Thus the valuation principles of heterodoxy and the continuity of the economic process are further compromised ' through changing patterns of scarcity and inequality, state formation, demographic transformation, and changing economic-socialisation. The examination of positive economics is a legitimate concern for macroeconomic theorists, as its ultimate objective is expressed in terms of policy evaluation.

However a causal deficiency in the political economic interpretation of macroeconomic analysis exists in a simultaneous system of relations, where the indirect effects of political policy may frustrate direct effects necessitating requantifications of macroeconomic theory. Additionally, there is seen to be collateral compromise amongst political objectives as subjective judgments concerning preferred combinations of policy are subjugated to empirical analysis. This is clearly unsatisfactory as it establishes misleading econometric policies through the implementation of models using estimated coefficients, if expectations are in turn rational.

It is within the context of the current crisis, of a discipline based on a cumulative premise of intellectual reason, that this rationalisation is concluded. As has been established in the opening chapters, economics as an intellectual discipline emerged in the seventeenth and eighteenth centuries. It was a substantial by-product of the philosophical revolution which inevitably created a distinctly 'modern' world. As a result, the concept of self-interest was liberated from theological contempt as a motive for human action, and evolved to be regarded as a precondition for a capitalist economy.

This process provided a reference point for a teleological progression. The obvious example is illustrated in the significance and originality of Adam Smith's *Wealth of Nations* which attempted to offer a rational explanation of why the proliferation of commercial transactions was morally defensible. Smith may be regarded as a primitive Newtonian in his conception of market phenomena that possessed an inherent order. However, the essential point is that the individuals pursuit of self interest in the marketplace produces unintentional consequences that are, on the whole, beneficial to everyone over time, hence the analogy of the 'invisible hand'. Smith perceived in the apparent chaos of the market place, a self-perpetuating economic order created by the participants as being the net result of Smith's own term. Therefore for the first time in history it became possible to conceptualise material progress for the human race as a reality, as opposed to an unachievable desire.

As a result of the acceptance of this rationalisation it became a moral imperative to structure 'objective laws' of the economic universe, in order to provide explanations of economic activity. It was further required that these laws could be expressed in a precise mathematical form in order to afford them perfect expression, and to establish a form of utility to provide political economic relevance.

This change in perspective created a change in economic perception from buoyant optimism to an oppressive blanket of pessimism. Writers such as Malthus and Ricardo served to exacerbate this situation with the establishment of several natural 'laws', so that by the mid-nineteenth century, economics was generally regarded by economists and laymen alike, as a science which as a priority was duty bound to uncovered natural 'iron laws' that ruled the economic universe. Therefore Smith's pan-economic universe actually constitutes the market place, and was replaced by a closed universe where human activity was restricted by a frigid and deterministic set of natural laws, indifferent to human aspirations. It is perhaps for this reason that the science of economics was perceived by people of literary sensibility to be an 'enemy' of humanity throughout the times of John Stuart Mill.

The Marginalist revolution, which occurred after 1870 sought to redress this problem of image by directing attention away from the distracting issues of the forbidding macro-models, into a new and equally complex model of the market place. The focus became the satisfaction of the wants and needs of the consumers and producers. This re-emphasis required the establishment of an ideal condition of 'equilibrium', where available resource were mobilised to best satisfy desires which were expressed in money prices. Within this context the 'pseudo-happiness' as it is described by contemporary European socialists, of the consumption society became the substance of political economics.

It is interesting to observe that the Maslovian distinction between wants and needs is little more than a secularised and pseudo-scientific version of the ancient distinction between our 'higher' and 'lower' selves. It is clearly a distinction that Smith, Ricardo, Malthus, Mill, Jevons, Walras and Keynes would never have repudiated. However it is evident that they did conclude that the practical application of economics theory is designed specifically to deal with the 'needs' of our 'higher selves and the 'wants' of our 'lower selves' which were previously the stewardship of philosophy and religion. This implies the belief that the 'lower' parts of ourselves, which represent self-interested impulses, are forever present and may never be totally repressed. Therefore within the context of the marketplace, the virtue of free commercial transactions between consenting adults, is that it directs impulses of self interest towards a simple common good; the general improvement of humanity's material condition.

The inevitable result of this development was the creation of a utilitarian calculus, capable of creating a mathematical application, as both an analytical and a descriptive tool, once a few simple axioms concerning the rationality of an 'economic man' were established. This facilitated an intellectual rigour that soon made it the envy of the other social sciences. Economics was subsequently defined as the rational allocation of scarce resources, where the economist strived to determine the logic of choice which would permit the development of a 'maximising' strategy.

This process took several forms, and the basic premise of economics was not affected by the 'Keynesian revolution'. As has been established, Keynes' originality lay in his overall economic conception of uncertainty within the economy, operating away from a position of equilibrium. The successful expansion of this theory enabled him to establish the premise of the reluctance of the price of labour to fall, when unemployment is widespread, as a permanent fact of a modern economy. He further argued that a money and credit economy was capable of propagating false signals to the businessman and the policy maker alike, which had the potential to result in a general glut, or depression. It is also relevant to mention that the subsequent incorporation of Keynesian insights into an elaborate, highly mathematical econometric model, in which elaborate correlations were sought among economic aggregates, might well have dismayed him.

The evident inadequacies of economic theory in consideration of the political application utility, which have been most obviously revealed in the policies derived from such theories over the past twenty years, have given rise to much dissent within the profession. However, it is worthy of note that the major dissenting paradigms have quite a bit in common. To begin with, as has been established, they all reject conventional Keynesian macroeconomics in its present form, and they adopt this attitude on similar grounds. Essentially it is argued that the prevalent econometric models of the economy are, in whole or in part 'scientific' simplifications of convenience seeking to interpret economic reality, which subsequently serves to mislead rather than illuminate. It is considered that such 'static' models are deficient in that their fundamental axiom of 'ceteris paribus' can never realistically apply to the real world of human action. Therefore instead of being 'scientific' they represent a form of mathematical manipulation, which attempt to mimic the physical sciences, but are in fact totally inadequate to achieve an understanding of the intricacies of human activity.

It is for this reason that the Post-Keynesians believe that 'dynamic models' based on economic aggregates are possible, and would be of sufficient theoretical resource to permit the economy as a whole to be 'planned' and 'managed' by the appropriate political economists. Other economists however, are highly sceptical of the meaningfulness of macroeconomic aggregates altogether, since their perspective on economic activity or 'radical subjectivism' is one that distrusts all economic statements that do not refer to something that is occurring in the minds of, and affecting the intentions and plans of, human factors.

Although the Post-Keynesians are highly critical of the scientific pretensions of modern economics, they still interpret the economy as a system organised along the same lines as those organised by natural forces, where the governing laws may be discerned by economists. This implies a rationalist view of the economic universe, but the rationalism is located within the individual, not within an entity labelled 'the economy'. Their 'methodological individualism' in economic reasoning is based on the 'self evident proposition present in every human mind'. The fact that humans acts purposefully and that any existential disparity between intent and result flows from an error of knowledge, implies that it is consistent within human nature for an individual to seek to improve his condition in the market place, and therefore by extension, capitalism is the only social system compatible with the nature of humanity.

For the dissident Radical economist, 'economic man' is a modern aberration. There exists a substantial moral revulsion against contemporary economics, and an equally powerful moral revulsion against contemporary capitalist society and the inherent economic theory with which it is associated. The Radical economist points out, for example, that economics tells you nothing about the moral and human quality of the 'universe' it attempts to explain. Of course

most economists would agree with this summation, but would hasten
to point out that this responsibility is more appropriately associated
with more relevant forms of human inquiry, such as political philosophy, theology etc, where the tasks of dealing with such normative
issues is well catered for.

The essence of the Radical attack, is therefore seen to reside in
the area of self-interest, the key human motivation in economics.
The Radical paradigm does not conclude that self-interest is an in-
expungible aspect of human endeavour, which conventional theory
seeks to come to terms with, though not necessarily to admire, and
ultimately to channel into constructive, or at least harmless activity.
Instead the Radical paradigm denies the premise, in an attempt to
dissolve economics into moral and political philosophy. The tactic
is derived from the psychological theories of the late Abraham Mas-
lov, who posited a universal hierarchy of natural human needs, as
opposed to subjective wants, and perceived human developments as
a progressive process of 'self actualisation', whereby human beings
become mature as they subordinate their particular selfish 'wants' to
deeper 'needs' whose satisfaction produces a community of autonomous, but no longer self-regarding persons.

The vision of Radical economics today is that of a democratic,
egalitarian community in which individual self-interests are to be
rendered as negligible through education, peer group pressure, and
a constant flow of elevating rhetoric; a simplified form of Utopian
socialism in modern academic guise. The fact that this line of reasoning should originate within the economic profession itself, yet
fails to incite a mass exodus, is a testimony to the intellectual confusion of the discipline. Further and a more important consideration
is that it emphasises the fundamental belief by sufficient supporters
of alternative paradigms, that the underlying premise of the Radical
interpretation of self-interest is far from acceptable.

Therefore if one accepts the belief that the study of economics
potentially constitutes one of the most scientific of all the social
sciences, where the body of theory concerning economic processes
is presented in a coherent formation, which once mastered, does

provide an 'expertise'; then it is necessary to accept the reality that there is a crisis within the practical application of macroeconomic theory. This is evident by the fact that the body of undisputed theory is shrinking out of proportion to that regarded by exponents of conflicting paradigms as being incontestable. It is increasingly obvious that the energies of economists seeking to establish themselves as authorities within the discipline, spend their time dissecting established theories, in the hope of gaining academic notoriety by virtue of their illuminating efforts in establishing controversy in almost every alternative theory.

It is clear from the evidence established through the body of this rationalisation that the conflicts within political-economic theory are not only varied and complex, but they are established to the point where there is a blurring of chronological relevance. This implies that once a contentious issue is established, it is not abolished or disproved, and therefore disregarded, but is employed to engender sufficient academic support to represent itself as a legitimate paradigm established in opposition to contemporary alternatives. Obviously a ground swell of opinion is all that is required to create numerous contentious paradigms, each representative of its own unique view of political reality, and those that subscribe to it. There can be little doubt that in view of this situation the 'science' of macroeconomics may be destined to forfeit its grandiose position within the social sciences, and be relegated to the back-lots of the more humanitarian academic endeavours.

It is appropriate to apportion a significant amount of the present crisis to the pretensions of the past. Indeed the current emphasis on 'revisionist' impulses would indicate that this is a reformist over-reaction, designed to reduce the scope of macroeconomic theory to that of the universally acceptable truths, as acknowledged by all parties. This may be interpreted as an attempt to shed the pseudo-scientific aspects of the discipline and thus reduce the parameters to that of the genuinely scientific, through an increased emphasis on quantitative econometric models; probably at the expense of any relevance to fundamental political economic reality.

Therefore the concept of macroeconomic theory would seem to be at an impasse in its development. The dominant quantitative model tends to represent an ever increasing distortion of economic reality, thus creating an ambiguous reference for political policy. However, as has become evident, the alternative paradigms are themselves contaminated with distinctive varieties of rationalism that establish their own impasse. The criticisms of the status quo in economics are well received, but the alternative proposals are far from convincing. There is no reason to believe that Post-Keynesians, attempting to fine tune their 'cybernetic' models, can do any better than Keynesians with their 'Newtonian-mechanical' model. Further the Radical economists have a rationalist-Utopian dream of a world in which individuals have transcended their inherent self-interest, that the process of economic activity may be done away with along with its conspirator, the market place.

Clearly the domains of economic preference continue to be monotonic as the social welfare function maps the profiles of individual preferences into social preferences or a set of alternatives assuming continuity, convexity or monotonicity of preferences, when really the preference profile lies in the 'economic domain'. Conditions which imply consistency against mean standard deviation and expected utility ranking or 'quadratic utility' combined with normally distributed random alternatives establish a credibility crises, for in reality, many economic models neither condition has theoretical support, nor do empirical tests for normality justify that restriction.

Yet macroeconomic theory survives the internal struggles for domination, and perhaps in fairness, the unreasonable demands that are imposed on it. It survives because the teleological developments in macroeconomic theory, as demonstrated within this investigation, have not only established the conflicting juxtapositions within the historical development, but it has also served to establish the existence of certain incontestable facts; within the realms of reason, from which certain Radical arguments are hereto discounted, that may serve to establish a base for future re-alignment of macroeconomic theory with macro-political economic reality.

The emphasis on the development of macroeconomic theory should rightfully reorientate its focus on the positive aspects of a discipline in crisis, which is still able to function, albeit in a contorted sense, and provide an acceptable accommodation of alternative realities. Admittedly the parameters of operational effectiveness tend to be abnormally distorted for an academic discipline seeking to maintain credibility in the face of abundant divisive internal considerations; however as it has been demonstrated, the differing emphasis on alternate macroeconomic characteristics has created a dispersal effect, as well as a cumulative foundation for economic theory to expand.

The inevitable result of the historical imperative development of a body of theory, which has the effect of reproducing conflicting and diverging paradigms from within the womb of the initial consideration, is to establish a discipline that is not only representative of the complete spectrum of political economic reality, but also to facilitate an eventual perception of fundamental economic truths in the context of rational expectation equilibrium.

An analysis of recursive stochastic algorithms demonstrates that a convergence to equilibrium and changing parameters when nonconvergence is indicated, establishes that in reality a self stabilising property eliminates the need to impose stability conditions on the economic environment. There is however, a requirement for a centralised forecasting mechanism, and a decentralised strategy adjusting process. Thus long run growth rates in capital consumption depends on tastes, technical factors, and policies. Therefore in a condition of free trade equilibrium with attendant taxation, it is considered that national growth rates of consumption and output need not converge. This affords increased credibility to the notion of a convex model of equilibrium, where technical and fixed factors contribute to consumption based asset pricing models, explicitly included in a time series behaviour of consumption and asset returns.

This facilitates an adaptive expectation hypothesis capable of utilising past forecasting errors to revise current expectations. Given the value of any variable X at time t this may then be expressed as

$_{t-1} x^e_t$ where individuals form expectations at the end of $_{t-1}$. An adaptive expectation hypothesis asserts that:

$$_{t-1} x^e_t - {}_{t-2}x^e_{t-1} = \Phi (x_{t-1} - {}_{t-2}x^e_{t-1}) \qquad 0 < \Phi < 1$$

Therefore by recursive substituting out unobserveable expectations with the inclusion of a forecasting error at time t-1 we may conclude:

$$_{t-1} x^e_t = \Phi x_{t-1} + \Phi (1 - \Phi) x_{t-2} + \Phi (1 - \Phi)^2 x_{t-3}$$

$$+ \dots + \Phi (1 - \Phi)^n x_{t-n-1}$$

$$+ (1 - \Phi)^{n+1} {}_{t-n-2} x^e_{t-n-1}$$

In this case all terms except the final term are observable, and since $(1-\Phi)^{n+1}$ gets steadily smaller as n is increased, Φ is a positive fraction. This then establishes a premise for a solution to the needs of both theoretical and empirical requirements, whereby expectation formulations may be adequately transcribed into a plausible behaviour assumption. An obvious application may be identified immediately through inflationary and nominal interest rate expectations, thus successfully facilitating the realistic injection of uncertainty into a classical stochastic model, as the essential structure of the problem remains the same. Therefore when the solution of a deterministic or non random model differs, future variables may be replaced by current expectations which must be said to exhibit certainty equivalence.

It is considered then, that the development of macroeconomic theory is best preserved from this translation deficiency by a form of hybrid development, capable of realistic and objective economic interpretation, which may access the relevant characteristics of the ample body of theoretical interpretations available, and therefore the establishment of a paradigm capable of effectively dealing with the economic anomalies of modern times. Any attempts at revisionist regression are considered to be counter productive to the macroeconomic objective of representing economic reality, as they conspire to disregard significant quantities of valuable research and insights that represent the theoretical foundations of the development of macroeconomic theory, as they apply to political economic considerations.

The numerous and well documented violations of expected utility theory equilibrium, further implies the existence of strict preferences between stochastically equivalent actions and implies certain systemic violations of monotonicity through regret theory aversion. However, the application of regret theory equates to an individually violate monotonicity.

Clearly it is essential that the direction of public policy be well targeted to the nature of the problem it is seeking to ameliorate, but only in the context of prudent, non-inflationary policies, because of the potential emergence of destructive dynamic forces as a result of the tensions inherent in the basic structure of the economy. The political economy is therefore subject to private sector maladjustments, given the propensity for misinterpretation due to structured property rights, the dual nature of capital, the interchangeable function of the financial system and the impact of investment spending on profit rates.

Therefore the political economy cannot be interpreted in a Neoclassical context, but must be examined within a systemic assessment of the political implications of an economic theory utilising appropriate simplifications to attempt to yield predictions that are not actually falsified by the underlying data. Thus the political parameters affect not only the policy equations in principle, but additionally attendant policy equations which may therefore be rendered inappropriate in simulating new policies. This may be expressed where mt denotes the logarithm of the nominal money stock as:

$$m_t = m_{t-1} + \theta$$

$$m_t = p_t + \alpha 1 - \alpha_2 \theta + \varepsilon_{1t} \quad \alpha 1 > 0 \quad \alpha 2 > 0$$

$$e_t = p^* - p_t$$

It is therefore necessary to conclude that an unequivocal refutation of the very basis of the hypothesis is questionable, as economists tend to look beyond the parameters of the paradigm itself by challenging the application of their theories as individual models dictating government behaviour are also evidently instrumental in forming expectations. In the event that the estimated coefficients of observable equations implicitly contain policy parameters which are construed as predicators of future actions, these political parameters will change when a new political policy is adopted. However it is clear that the relevance of macroeconomic theory may prove to be more intractable when the object is not to test the political expectation assumptions, but rather to test the assumption relevant to the underlying economic structure.

Bibliography

Balogh, T.: *The Irrelevance of Contemporary Economics*, Weidenfeld and Nicolson, 1982.

Barber, W. J.: 'Alfred Marshall and the Framework of Neo-Classical Economics', in *A History Of Economic Thought*.

Barclay, W. J. Jr. and Stengel, M.: 'Surplus and Surplus Value', *Review of Radical Political Economy*, Number 1, 1977.

Baron, P. and Sweezy, P. M.: *Monopoly Capital*, Pelican, 1968.

Blaug, M. Adam Smith: *Economic Theory in Retrospect*, Heinemann. Chapter 2, 1968.

Cambridge Journal of Economics, Volume 15, Cambridge Political Economy Society, Academic Press, London, 1991.

Chick, V: *Inflation from a Longer Term Perspective: Lessons from the General Theory*, University of London, 1983.

Chick, V: 'The Nature of the Keynesian Revolution: A Reassessment'. *Australian Economic Papers*, volume 17, June 1978, Number 30. p. 17.

Chick, V: *Macroeconomics After Keynes*, University of London, Philip Allan, 1983.

Clower, R. W.: 'The Keynesian Counterrevolution; A Theoretical Appraisal', in F. H. Hahn and F. P. R. Brechling, editors, *The Theory of Interest Rates*, Macmillan, 1965.

Coddington, A.: Keynesian Economics: A Search For First Principles, in *Journal of Economics*, Volume XIV, December 1976.

Dalton, D: *Primitive, Archaic and Modern Economies, Essays of Karl Polanyi*, Doubleday, Anchor Books, 1968.

Eatwell, J.: *Keynes's Economics and the Theory of Value and Distribution*, Duckworth, London, 1983.

149

Economica. 'Are Preferences Monotonic? Testing Some Predictions Of Regret Theory', London School Of Economics, Volume 59, Number 233, February 1992.

Economic Inquiry. *The Journal of Western Economics Association International*, Huntington Beach, California, January 1991.

Economic Review. Volume 28, Number 2, Second Quarter, Federal Reserve Bank of Cleveland, 1992.

Edwards, R.: 'A Radical Approach To Economics', *American Economic Review*, 1970.

Edwards, R., MacEwan, A. et al: 'A Radical approach to Economics: Basis for a New Curriculum', *American Economic Review*, Volume 60. number 2, May 1970.

Ekelund, R. Jr: *A History of Economic Theory and Method*, McGraw Hill, 1975. G. R. Feel Kalecki: 'Contribution Over Four Decades'. Tiwel: 'Issues in the Economic Theory of Capitalism and Socialism; Michael Kalecki's Contribution Over Four Decades.' *The Indian Economic Journal*, Volume XX, Number 2, October–December 1972.

Franklin: *American Capitalism: Two Visions*, Chapter 7.

Friedman, M.: *Introduction Capitalism and Freedom*, Chicago, 1962.

Friedman, M.: The Counter-Revolution in Monetary Theory. Institute of Economics affairs, Occasional Paper 33, 1970.

Friedman, M.: 'The Quantity Theory of Money – A Restatement', in M. Friedman (ed.), *Essays in the Quantity Theory of Money* Chicago, Chicago University Press, 1956.

Friedman, M.: *Capitalism and Freedom*, University of Chicago Press, and extracts reprinted in Romano and Leiman, Second Edition.

Friedman, M.: 'Demand for Money; Some Theoretical and Empirical Results', *Journal of Political Economy*, 1959. Reprinted as Occasional Paper 68, New York, National Bureau Of Economic Research, 1959.

Fusfield, D: *The Age of The Economist*, University of Michigan, New York, 1972.

Gaibraith, J. K.: *American Capitalism*, Penguin, 1963.

Gaibraith, J. K.: *Economics and the Public Purpose*, Pelican, 1975.

Gambs, J. S.: *John Kenneth Galbraith*, Twayne, 1975.

Gill, R.: 'The Evolution of Modern Economics', *Classical Economics*, Prentice Hall, 1967.

Giahe, F. R. and Lee, D. R.: *Microeconomics, Theory and Application*, Harcourt Brace and Jovanovich International Edition, New York, 1981.

Gordan, S.: 'The Close of the Galbraithian System', *Journal of Political Economy*, July–August, 1968.

Hailstones, T. J.: *Economics, An Analysis of Principles and Policies*, Second Edition, South-West Publishing Company, Brighton, 1975.

Harcourt, G.: *Some Cambridge Controversies in the Theory of Capital*, Cambridge University Press, 1972.

Heilbroner, R.: *The Wordly Philosopher* (See also Heilbroner's The Making of Economic Society)

Heilbroner, R.: *The Making of Economic Society*, Fourth Edition, Prentice-Hall, 1972.

Heilbroner, R.: 'The Wonderful World of Adam Smith', *The Wordly Philosphers*.

Hicks, J. R.: 'Mr Keynes and the Classics, A Suggested Interpretation', *Econometrica*. Volume 5, 1937.

Hobsbawm, E.: *Industry and Empire*, Pelican, 1969.

Hobson, J. A.: 'Economic Heretic', *American Journal of Economics and Sociology*, July 1978.

Hughes, J.: *Industdrialisation and Economic History: Theses and Coniectures*, McGraw-Hill, 1970.

Hunt, E. K. and Sherman, H. J.: *Economics: An Introduction to Traditional and Radical Views*, Harper and Row, 1972.

Johnson, H. G.: 'The General Theory After Twenty-Five Years', *American Economic Review*, May, 1961.

Kaldor: 'Alternative Theories of Distribution', *Revolutionary Economic Studies*, 1956. Reprinted in Kaldor, Essays on Value and Distribution, London, Duckworth, 1960.

Kalecki, M.: *Selected Essays on the Dynamics of the Capitalist Economy*, Cambridge, Cambridge University Press, 1971; and *Selected Essays on the Economic Growth of the Socialist and Mixed Economy*, Cambridge, Cambridge University Press, 1972.

Kalecki, M.: 'Trend and Business Cycles Reconsidered', *Economic Journal*, June 1968 p. 265. Reprinted in Selected Essays on the Dynamics of the Capitalist Economy.

Keynes, J. M.: *The General Theory of Employment Interest and Money*, Macmillan, 1936.

Keynes, J. M.: *The End of Laissez-Faire*, London, Macmillan, 1936.

Keynes, J. M.: *On The Theory of a Monetary Economy*, Duncker and Humbolt, Munich, 1933.

Keynes, J. M.: *The General Theory and After, Part II Defence and Developments*, Macmillan, 1973.

Keynes, J. M.: 'The General Theory of Employment', *Quarterly Journal of Economics*, February, 1937.

Kirzner, M.: *The Economic Point of View*, Sheed and Ward, Kansas, 1970.

Kristol, I.: 'A Disabled Science', *The Age Monthly Review*, Vol. 1, No. 2, 1981.

Kregei, J. A.: *An Introduction to Post-Keynesian Economics*, Macmillan, Hong Kong, 1973.

Kregel, J. A.: *The Reconstruction of Political Economy: An Introduction to Post-Keynesian Economics*, New York, Wiley, Halsted Press, 1973, Chapter 11.

Kregel, J. A.: 'Economic Methodology in the Face of Uncertainty: The Modelling Methods of Keynes and the Post-Keynesians.' *The Economic Journal*, June 1976, volume 86. Number 342. p. 220.

Komaj, J.: *Anti-equilibrium: On Economic Systems Theory and the Tasks of Research*, New York, American Eisevier, Amsterdam and London, North Holland, 1971.

Kuhn, T. S.: *The Structure of Scientific Revolutions*, Chicago. University of Chicago Press, 1962.

Leach, J.: 'Rational Speculation', *The Journal of Political Economy* (University of Chicago) Volume 99, Number 1, February 1991

Lekachman, R.: 'Adam Smith', *A History of Economic Ideas*, McGraw Hill, 1959, Chapter 4.

Lekachman, R.: *Harper's*, Volume 254, Number 1521, February 1977. pp. 35–40.

Leijonhufvud, A.: *On Keynesian Economics and the Economics of Keynes*, Oxford University Press, 1968.

Leijonhufvud, A.: Keynes and the Classics, The Institute of Economic Affairs – Occasional Paper 30.

Lindbeck, A.: *The Political Economy of the New Left: an Outsiders View.*

Murad, A.: *What Keynes Means*, Bookman Associates, New York, 1962.

Olson, M. Jr: 'What is Economics?' in J. H. Weaver, *Modern Political Economy: Radical and Orthodox Views on Crucial Issues*, Allyn and Bacon, 1973.

Oser, J.: *The Evolution Of Economic Thought*, Syracuse University, New York, 1970.

Patinkin, D. and Leith, J. C.: *Keynes, Cambridge and The General Theory*, The University of Ontario, 1977.

Polanyi, K.: The Great Transformation, reprinted in Dalton. Robbins: *The Theory of Economic Policy in English Classical Political Economy*, Macmillan, 1952.

Preston, N. S.: *Politics, Economics and Power*, Macmillan, 1967.

The Review of Radical Political Economics. Volume 2. The Union For Radical Political Economics, University of California, Riverside, California. Winter 1989.

The Review of Radical Political Economics. Volume 22, Number 4. The Union For Radical Political Economics, University of California, Riverside, California. Winter 1990.

Reynolds, L. G. Economics. *A General Introduction*, Richard D Irwin, Inc. Homewood, Illinois. Third Edition, 1969.

Richmond, W. H.: *Jevons, Sidgwick and Marshall on the Role of the State in Economic Activity*, University of Queensland, 1982, Inclusive.

Richmond, W. H.: *Political Economy and Comparitive Systems*, 1985. p. 3.

Robinson, J.: *The Generalisation of the General Theory*, St. Martin's Press, New York, 1979.

Robinson, J.: *The Rate of Interest and Other Essays*. London, Macmillan, 1952.

Robinson, J.: 'The second crises of Economic Theory', *The American Economic Review*, Volume XXI. Number 3.

Robinson, J.: *The Accumulation of Capital*, London, Macmillan, 1956. pp. 404–406.

Robson, J. M. (ed.): *Principles of Political Economy*, Book V, University of Toronto Press, 1965.

Romano, R. and Leiman: 'Adam Smith's Wealth Of Nations', in *Views On Capitalism*, Glencoe, 1975.

Samuelson, P. A.: 'Strengths of a Mixed Economy', *Economic Impact*, Number 36, 1984.

Samuelson, P. A.: *Economics*, Second Australian Edition, Sydney, McGraw-Hill Book Company, 1955.

Seligman, B.: *Main Currents in Modern Economics*, Quadrangle Books, Chicago, 1971.

Solow, R. M.: 'The New Industrial State or Son of Affluence', *The Public Interest*: Number 9, 1967.

Sweezy, P. M.: 'Utopian Reformism', *Monthly Review*, November, 1973.

Taylor, A. J.: *Laissez-Faire and State Intervention in the Nineteenth Century Britain*.

The Journal of Political Economy. Volume 98, Number 4. University of Chicago. February–December 1990.

The Journal of Political Economy. Volume 98, Number 1. University of Chicago. February 1990.

The Journal of Political Economy. Volume 99, Number 1. University of Chicago. February 1991.

The Journal of Political Economy. Volume 99, Number 2. University of Chicago. April 1991.

The Journal of Economic Issues. Urban Economics and Economic Heterodoxy. Volume 24. March 1990.

The Journal of European Economic History. Volume 20, Number 3. Banco Di Roma, Rome. Winter 1991.

Tobin, J.: 'The Monetary Interpretation of History', *American Economic Review*, 1965.

Tobin, J.: 'Money and Income: Post Hoc Ergo Propter Hoc?', *Quarterly Journal of Economics*, 1970.

Veblen, T.: *The Theory of Business Enterprise, Romano and Leiman, Views on Capitalism.*

Viner, J.: 'Adam Smith and Laissez-Faire', *Journal of Political Economy*, Volume 35.1927.

Ward, B.: *What's Wrong With Economics?*, Macmillan, 1972.

Waters, W. J. and Wheelright, E. L.: 'University Economics – a Radical Critique', from E. L. Wheelwright and Frank J. B. Stilwell (eds.), *Readinqs in Political Economy*, Volume 1, ANZ Book Company, 1976.